Praise for the
OPEN YOUR HEART series

*"*It's a great idea!*"*

—Regis Philbin

*"*The OPEN YOUR HEART series
is a winning combination
that both instructs and inspires.*"*

—Hazel Dixon-Cooper, author of *Born On a Rotten Day*
and *Love On a Rotten Day*, and *Cosmopolitan
Magazine*'s Bedside Astrologer

*"*The perfect books to improve your mind,
get in shape, and find inspiration.*"*

—Bonnie Hearn Hill, author of *Intern, Killer Body*,
and the Geri LaRue newspaper thriller series

OPEN YOUR HEART
with *Writing*

Mastering Life through Love of Words

NEIL M. ROSEN

DreamTime Publishing, Inc.

DreamTime Publishing, Inc., books are available at special quantity discounts for bulk purchases for sales promotions, premiums, fund-raising, and educational needs. Please contact us at www.DreamTimePublishing.com for additional information.

Library of Congress Cataloging-in-Publication Data

Rosen, Neil M.
  Open your heart with writing : mastering life through love of words / Neil M. Rosen.
   p. cm.
  Includes bibliographical references and index.
  ISBN-13: 978-1-60166-008-4 (trade pbk.)
  1. Authorship—Psychological aspects. I. Title.

PN171.P83R67   2007
808'.02019—dc22   2007016069

Branding, website, and cover design for DreamTime Publishing by
   Rearden Killion • www.reardenkillion.com
Illustrations by Janice Marie Phelps • www.janicephelps.com
Manuscript consulting by Jeannette Cézanne • www.customline.com
Text layout and design by Gary A. Rosenberg • www.garyarosenberg.com

This publication is designed to provide accurate and authoritative information in regard to the subject matter covered. It is sold with the understanding that the publisher is not engaged in rendering legal, accounting, or other professional service. If legal advice or other expert assistance is required, the services of a competent professional person should be sought.
   —From a declaration of principles jointly adopted by a committee of the American Bar Association and a committee of publishers

This book is printed on recycled, acid-free paper containing a minimum of 50% recycled, de-inked fiber.

Contents

Note from the Publisher, vii

Acknowledgments, ix

Introduction, 1

ONE

The Journey Begins, 5

THE WRITING EXPERIENCE:
Copycat, Copycat, 10

TWO

Girls, 13

THE WRITING EXPERIENCE:
The Archaeology of the Mind, 18

Some Thoughts on Writing . . .
from Richard Lewis, 19

THREE

Wheels, 23

THE WRITING EXPERIENCE:
There's More Than One Way
to Find a Story, 29

FOUR

Wordsworth, Keats, Byron,
and Shelley, 31

THE WRITING EXPERIENCE:
Stop, Look, and Listen, 38

FIVE

The Circus Comes to Town, 41

THE WRITING EXPERIENCE:
Jacks or Better to Open, 48

SIX

Nota Bene: Note Well, 51

THE WRITING EXPERIENCE:
Note Well, 58

Some Thoughts on Writing . . .
from Katherine Hall Page, 59

SEVEN
It Takes One
to Know One, 63

THE WRITING EXPERIENCE:
Almost Animals, 73

EIGHT
Open Your Heart with
Writing, 75

THE WRITING EXPERIENCE:
When You Have Something
to Say, Write it Down, 82

NINE
Writing is a Relative
Experience, 85

THE WRITING EXPERIENCE:
Putting Google to Work
for You!, 93

Some Thoughts on Writing . . .
from Elaine Gottlieb, 96

TEN
Teach What You Learn, 99

THE WRITING EXPERIENCE:
Photo Ops, 107

ELEVEN
What Moves at the Speed
of Thought?, 109

THE WRITING EXPERIENCE:
A Lesson in Business
Writing, 122

Some Thoughts on Writing . . .
from Austin Boyd, 123

TWELVE
You Write What You Are, 129

THE WRITING EXPERIENCE:
Get on Your Hobby Horse, 137

THIRTEEN
Memories Are Made
of This, 139

THE WRITING EXPERIENCE:
The Loudest Day
in America, 147

FOURTEEN
When Two People Think
Alike, 149

THE WRITING EXPERIENCE:
Blogging with the Authors, 156

Resources, 159

Index, 167

About the Author, 171

Note from the Publisher

Balancing the overall mission of a series of books with each author's individual creativity and vision is an enjoyable and rewarding challenge. The goal of this note is to tie the loose ends together to make your experience with this book as meaningful as possible.

We have two goals with the Open Your Heart series. The first is to provide you with practical advice about your hobby or interest, in this case writing. We trust this advice will increase your ongoing enjoyment of putting pen to paper (fingers to keyboard), or even encourage you to explore a new side of yourself as yet undiscovered.

Our second goal is to help you use what you know and love to make the rest of your life happier and easier. This process worked in different ways for each of our writers, so it will likely work in different ways for each of you. For some, it's a matter of becoming more self-aware. Just realizing what makes you happy when you're writing, and then gradually learning to use those feelings as a barometer when dealing with your job, relationships, and other issues could be an important first step. For others, writing provides an important outlet for stress and contemplation, allowing you to go back into your daily life refreshed. For yet others, you might discover how to meditate, how to connect with the mysterious flow of the Universe when you are immersed in writing, journaling, or the many other ways you can create with the written word. Once you recognize the beauty of that for what it is, you can then learn to connect with the flow in other ways at other times.

We are not suggesting you will find all of your answers in this book. We are, though, inviting you to look at something you love with new eyes, a new perspective, and a new heart. Once you recognize the importance of feeling good in one area of your life, you are open to feeling good in the rest of your life. And that is the cornerstone to mastering your life.

Happy reading!

Meg Bertini

Meg Bertini
Publisher

Acknowledgements

I want to thank my wife Roseann, whose patience is monumental. Starting from the day 30 years ago when I came home at lunch to tell her I had quit my job, right up to the present time, her support has been unwavering and has helped me explore whatever road my heart traveled. On that day, the first time in our relationship that I changed jobs, she sat with our first child in her arms, only a year old, and told me it would work out just fine for us. It seems that, on top of patience, she had the ability to see into the future.

I'd also like to thank Gail Simpson for all the years we have known each other and worked together on various writing projects, inspiring each other to keep writing when the original inspiration had worn off a bit. And I'd like to thank all of my friends and family who put up with me when my writing mind goes off on its own and keeps me out of touch for a while.

To my friend and editor Jeannette Cézanne, without whom this book would never have been written, I give special thanks. Finally I would like to thank Meg Bertini, my publisher, for all of her support and hard work in developing the Open Your Heart book series and this book in particular.

This book is dedicated to my children,
Kara, Daniel, and Jenna

Mixed Messages

If I send you
Mixed messages

It's only because
I want you to take risks
Yet always be safe

Experience love
But avoid the pain
That comes with the territory

Enjoy life's struggles
Without struggling

And find happiness
Without having to search
Under too many rocks

I want you to
Learn from my mistakes
Not your own

Have the courage
To live up to your convictions
But not have to prove it

Know who you are
Without settling, and
Without exploring your dark side

Be in touch with your feelings
While remaining strong

And be more than I am
Without being less than you can be

I want you to
Find your own way
Using my map

And make your own mistakes
Guilt free

And I know that
It is in the very wanting
Of what I want for you

I pave a road
Rife with confusion and conflict,
    and
Mixed messages

Introduction

If I don't write to empty my mind,
I go mad.
—LORD BYRON

I'm driving south on I-95, heading to the Delaware shore for a week's vacation.

The school year just ended, and after spending the past ten months in a classroom filled with fourth- and fifth-graders, my mind needs to get clear. The car is full of family, my wife with me in the front and the three kids sitting in the back, driving us crazy . . . as is their natural obligation.

An hour into the four-and-a-half-hour trip things calm down— the silence broken intermittently by random snoring. One child is sleeping, another listening to music through his headphones, and the third alternates between reading and asking how close we are to our destination. My wife is dozing; I insisted that we leave at five in the morning to avoid traffic and get an early jump on the vacation. It will be a bonus, I feel, to be already vacationing when the other families joining us for the week arrive.

Others in my family, at the moment, would probably disagree.

Driving, I let my mind wander. I don't actually have a whole lot of choice in the matter. Free will is a myth. I am a writer when I am awake and when I am asleep, and especially when I am in that special place between the two where I am now, when my mind goes off in search of material and there isn't a thing I can do about it.

Writing is unequal parts joy and frustration. I experience creative explosions seconds before mind-numbing emptiness, like watching streaming media on your computer one moment and having a broken Internet connection the next. The emotional roller coaster challenges your mind and strikes directly at your heart.

Frequently, while driving, I become so engrossed in thought that my consciousness is out of touch with what is happening on the surface of the planet, and when that happens I can drive miles past my intended exit, or arrive at an unintended destination (as I did once when I pulled into the driveway of a house I hadn't lived in for fifteen years). Luckily, whatever part of me I leave behind to drive the car adroitly avoids collisions and never lets me run out of gas.

My college statistics professor employed a full-time chauffeur to drive him to and from the university—this at a time when college teachers were grossly underpaid. He had no choice in the matter. In the past, driving on his own, he had become so lost that it took him hours to find his way home.

His explanation? He'd started counting the telephone poles on the side of the road and measuring the distance between them by driving at a steady speed and counting the seconds it took to go from one to the next; soon he was using that information to figure out how many poles there were per square mile, how many there were in the state, the country, the world, the solar system, the galaxy . . . He ended up hopelessly lost, every time.

Everyone used to say that the poor man was absentminded. That must mean that I'm absentminded too, I guess. People talk about absentmindedness as if it were, somehow, a problem. Those people have obviously never tried it! It's actually a wonderful thing for the mind to go off and have an uninterrupted chance to make sense of the assorted flotsam and jetsam it has collected over a period of weeks and months and years.

My mind starts by taking a leisurely stroll through the archives, peeking under boxes, into filing cabinets, behind walls, and in desk drawers, leaving no stone unturned. At some point, it latches on to a gold nugget, an archived thought, event, picture, or puzzle, and won't let go. Now the stroll is over, and its time to get down to serious business.

I am in the process of writing my next book, musical, poem or song, organizing notes in my head, preparing a business plan, or creating marketing campaigns. I'm talking to future characters, getting to know them, visiting the scene of the crime to be sure I have the details right, and tracking multiple plots to their less-than-obvious conclusions.

The only sure thing is that whatever is going on in my head will be on my hard drive one day soon. I have no control over that. If I don't get it on paper and out of my head, it will haunt me *ad infinitum.*

By the time I do sit down at my desk and write, the words flow easily, the characters have been mostly developed, the scene set, and the story line plotted. The need to write started in my heart, then got lost in my head for weeks, months, or even years . . . but eventually my mind made sense of it and sent it back to my heart, where confirmation created the obsession. The obsession to write.

Now as I near the end of the New Jersey Turnpike, my mind drifts closer to the surface, possibly because I sense someone in the car talking to me.

I slowly come up, still deep in thought, and hear a second voice interrupt the first.

"Don't you see how Dad's mouth is moving, the way he's puffing out his cheeks?" It is the voice of my oldest child, already very aware of the world around her. "See how his lips are pursed? Don't you know? That means he isn't here right now. So there's no use trying to get his attention. Wait until the puffing stops before you try and talk to him."

I drift away again, my mind smiling.

ONE

The Journey Begins

Perhaps imagination is only intelligence having fun.

—GEORGE SCIALABBA

They came again last night.

It's what they do. They wait for the house to be quiet; I realize that it's been quiet for a while. The noises my parents make walking, cleaning up, watching television, talking, and finally locking the doors, have stopped. They've gone to bed. The only sounds you hear now are those being made by my sisters and me, whispering to each other from our bedrooms across the hall upstairs in our Long Island home. My voice is more urgent than theirs, because I am motivated, trying to put off the inevitable. "Let's talk about something," I say. "What do you want to talk about?"

"I don't care. Anything," says my younger sister. "What do you want to talk about?"

"Shh!" cautions our older sister.

The conversation dies before it starts; soon their voices drift away as they fall asleep, and I turn, resigned, to my pillow.

Maybe I drift off, maybe not. But when they come, whether it's five minutes or two hours later, I'm awake. I won't sleep again for a while.

They aren't exactly threatening, but I'm still not about to allow them free run of the room. Their presence requires me to be awake while they explore the room, sometimes settling in one place for a while, other times rushing to and fro. They are more interested in each other than they are in me, but they must have chosen my room for a reason. Now one perches lightly on the foot of my bed while the other sits on my dresser directly across the room. They look at each other, ignoring me totally.

I share the space under my covers with friends of a different sort, and I turn to them every night when I get into bed, or when I wake up early with time to spare, or whenever *they* are there and I can't sleep. Franklin W. Dixon, Victor Appleton, Clair Bee, and Carolyn Keene, among others, nestle comfortably against me as I lie in bed, waiting to be read.

Sometimes I turn over and knock one of my favorite books off the bed in the middle of the night. It falls with a loud thud on the hardwood floor, waking my father in the bedroom below. When that happens, he trudges up the stairs to my room to be sure it's not me falling out of bed, and he stands in the doorway for a few minutes to see if I am sleeping. I lie in bed as quietly as possible until I know he's back in his own bed and asleep.

He teases me about it the next day at breakfast, in front of my giggling sisters, joking that I'd fallen out of bed in the middle of the night yet again, but that by the time he came to my rescue I had climbed back in and was asleep. But Dad saw the books on the floor, and smiles knowingly at my guilty face as he tells the story. Thankfully, he never asks me to remove the books from beneath my covers.

I am only eight, still a year or two away from Isaac Asimov, Jules Verne, H.G. Wells, and Samuel Clemens.

I also hide a flashlight under my pillow with extra batteries close by, just in case. In the quiet of the night, I lie on my back and tent the covers by raising my knees, or by using the Louisville Slugger I keep next to the bed to create a bigger tent. It's carefully constructed, designed to give me room to read while keeping light from escaping to the hallway and into my sisters' room—there are no closed doors in my house. Quickly, I lose myself in adventure sports, science fiction, and mystery, until finally my mind becomes quiet, and I forget about my friends, and sleep descends.

By the age of nine, I read faster than all my author friends combined could publish, devouring one book after another, reading every book in every series to which I was addicted. I added new series to the mattress collection when I came across them, but I never read a book twice; that was against the law—my law.

Of course, the libraries were full of books, most of which I never looked at (even though many were recommended by my parents, or were on the school's "must read" list for third-graders). Later I would read many of them and enjoy their wonder, but at nine, I had "my" friends and I was pretty inflexible. I didn't want to learn from books, I wanted to be entertained, kept on the edge of my seat; I wanted the good guys to win, every time.

The day came, inevitably, when I finished one of the stories and realized there were no more unread books from my favorite authors under my covers.

The first time that happened, I spent hours in the library, leafing through each book in each series to see if there might be an old book I had overlooked. I read the first few pages of each until I satisfied myself that I had, indeed, already read it. I had even caught up on the early books in each series, those written before I was born or before I learned to read. There were simply no unread books, and going to bed that night—or any night—without a new book under my covers simply wasn't an option.

The way I saw it, I had two choices. I could risk trying to find a new author, a new series that I could start that very day . . . or I could write my own.

I decided I would write my own.

Being pragmatic, even at the age of nine, I decided not to completely write my own book, but instead my own Franklin W. Dixon mystery. I didn't need characters—I already had them: good guys, bad guys, and a supporting cast of hundreds. Didn't need settings; I had them too. Dixon had already written all that for me.

All I needed was a plot—and there is nothing a nine-year-old with a fertile imagination has if not a plot. In my books, there were great riches stashed in deserted houses, overturned boats, and school lockers. There was a labyrinth beneath the school that stayed with me through every Hardy Boys book I wrote. And I prided myself in always having the simplest of clues lead to the case being solved, and the bad guys being locked up: Clues like a bike that had been moved from one side of the alley to the other, an unmade bed, a flat tire, and a cat door that wouldn't open.

The pages flew by as I wrote. Within weeks I had written over two hundred pages of a Hardy Boys mystery that was so good it would have made you cry. Another week and my first book was finished, signed on the cover page, and neatly stashed under my bed. I read that book over and over, making minor changes, but mostly keeping it indelibly etched in my mind. I believe I captured the essence of Dixon's heroes in that story, and created an intricate plot of my own that kept the reader hanging right up to the last page.

No one saved my first Hardy Boys book, or any that came after, or my first science-fiction thriller, *Chip Hilton Saves the Day* sports thriller, or the Nancy Drew novel I wrote once I reconciled myself to writing a book where the hero was a girl.

Now I read books, and I wrote books, every night. When I had a new book to read I still found time each evening to write a few pages, and when I ran out of unread books, I wrote—hundreds of pages at a time, always in pencil, always on a yellow pad. My bed became more and more crowded. Under my covers were not only books and a flashlight and batteries, but also lots of writing pads and pencils. The nights were rare when something or other didn't fall out of my bed, and hit the floor with a thud. My father had by then stopped trudging up the stairs to check on me. Some nights I read, some nights I wrote, and most nights I did both, but clearly my love for writing had caught up to my love for reading.

It was really about developing self-confidence. Each time I completed a book and signed my name on the cover, I felt ready to write another. In spite of a nine-year-old's dreams of grandeur, none of my books got published, and after giving the first one to my parents to read, and getting a positive "how nice" response, without either of them actually reading it, I never shared my books with anyone. My fantasy was to send my books to the authors who inspired them, positive that if they *just read the book* they would co-publish it with my name on the cover along with theirs, but I didn't do that either. I didn't have to. Writing was rewarding enough.

Seeing "The End" on that last page after the mystery was solved and the bad guys were locked away never failed to make my heart jump.

Writing saved me from feeling like a failure when my grades in school didn't come up to expectations, and writing kept me company through my longest nights.

My "early period" lasted two years, ending when I graduated from elementary school at the age of ten. In junior high school, I got addicted to sports: Baseball, basketball, football, it didn't matter. I was also addicted to riding my bicycle from one end of town to the other to visit friends and was making my initial foray into entrepreneurship with my very own newspaper delivery route. Add to this the hours I spent fidgeting in school each day and it's easy to see that I no longer had a problem falling asleep at night. And, as I mentioned earlier, I discovered Samuel Clemens, Isaac Asimov, Jules Verne, and H.G. Wells . . . and other monumental writers who intimidated me enough that I would never consider stealing their characters.

Did I mention that my night visitors moved on? I have only a vague memory as to whether they provoked fear in my eight-year-old mind, and if their antics kept me awake at night. Should I credit them for having turned me into a writer? I'd like to think not, but I wouldn't bet against it.

At the end of the day, I do owe *them* thanks: In their own way they introduced me to writing, an avocation that has sculpted, in one way or another, every stage of my life, and protected me from demons more real and more threatening than they ever were.

In case you are interested, I didn't start writing again until I discovered girls.

The Writing Experience

Part 1: Copycat, Copycat

A great way to develop writing skills is to use content from your favorite authors as a template for your writing. This technique is flexible and easy to make part of your writing schedule. It will help you develop skills in every area of the writing experience, from plot to character development to setting the scene.

As a nine-year-old, I used the books of Franklin W. Dixon and others to develop my writing skills, focusing on plot development. I didn't have to think about developing characters or settings (Dixon did that for me),

A Well-Known Television Series

and that allowed me to focus on the area of writing where I felt most comfortable.

To this day I use similar techniques to develop other aspects of my writing ability. For example, I develop a character of my own and insert it seamlessly into an existing book, or story, or episode of a television show I enjoy. I describe the character and the character's role in the story, develop the character's relationship to the other characters in the book or show, and after that write a new story or episode where my character plays an important, if not major, role.

Another technique I use is to take a well-known television series and have it take place in a new location. When you combine research and your own original ideas to create a new location, it is interesting to see the influence it has on changing the dynamics of a story.

When I write poetry I "practice" by replacing the last stanza of a poem I love with one of my own, or sometimes add an entirely new stanza to the poem. I do the same thing with songs, adding a verse to an existing song. (This is easy because I frequently can't understand the words to songs I hear on the radio and make up my own, anyway!)

Use the works of authors you cherish to improve your writing skills. Whether to improve your character-development skills or develop other aspects of your writing, building new skills or enhancing those you already have, these techniques will prove valuable. Never be afraid to use the great works of authors you admire to help take your writing to another level.

TWO

Girls

A writer's mind seems to be situated partly
in the solar plexus and partly in the head.
—ETHEL WILSON

I started writing again when I discovered girls.

Notice that there is nothing reciprocal in that sentence. Starting in seventh grade, a writer's lifetime from the Hardy Boys, I reinvented myself as the most prolific writer of schoolboy notes in the history of public education. According to the only person to read those notes—the source—there were cute notes, clever notes, and long drawn-out notes, each proclaiming my love, my desire to take a girl to a dance or prom, or even an unlikely low-value offer to help with homework.

My notes were beautifully penned. Friends, family, and teachers, all reported that for a boy, my handwriting was outstanding. Looking at the handwriting of the other boys in my class, however, dulled the compliments. What constituted outstanding handwriting for boys and made mine stand out was simply that it was legible.

In addition to being beautifully written, all my notes had another thing in common. They never were delivered to the intended recipient, the girl sitting next to me, or behind me in the classroom. In fact, delivering them was never more than a passing consideration. The notes were a necessary evil that enabled me to fight boredom and continue writing. At the end of each class my notes wound up torn into bits and deposited in the circular file, never to be read—and, more importantly, never to surface unexpectedly to embarrass me.

Although I never passed a note to anyone, I still managed to get in trouble for these creative efforts. I remember specifically the time my history teacher was wandering around the classroom as he gave his lecture, and I was lost in my note writing. Oblivious to my surroundings, I got caught red-handed. He picked a note up off my desk and I had a real fear that he was about to end my life and read it to the class, but after looking at it for a few seconds, my prayers were answered and he put it back, but not before telling me to remain after school for detention.

After school, head down, eyes diverted, we met in detention hall as requested and he let me know in no uncertain terms that I couldn't "pass" notes in class: I needed to pay attention, read the required materials, and study, in order to "pass" the class. He was right, of course, and off to detention I went.

I never told my teacher that I was being punished for the one thing I couldn't possibly do—*pass* notes in class. I could write them all day long, in the classroom, on the bus, and in my room at home when I was supposed to do my homework. I could ignore teachers, disassociate from all classroom activities. But actually pass my notes on to a girl? Never.

Today, having been a teacher myself, it's easy to relate to how frustrated my teachers were with my seeming lack of effort, mediocre grades, and lack of motivation. They were as confused as my parents and the other "professionals" they enlisted to help them understand why I wasn't performing to my potential.

Of course there was no thought given at the time that in one area, writing, I might be performing *above* my potential. In English class, time and emphasis were spent teaching spelling, grammar, and vocabulary, all of which I found boring: No one seemed particularly interested in *what* was written—in the actual content.

To receive an A in English, you handed in neatly written papers of the expected length with no spelling or grammatical errors, and *voilà*, your A appeared. The content was irrelevant. I got my only Bs and As in high school English, because it came easier to me than geography, Latin, or chemistry . . . not because I found it more interesting or worked harder.

My only saving grace was that I was pre-let's-diagnose-every-child-who-doesn't-perform-to-expectations with some-sort-of-ADD, and I only had to live with being a daydreamer, lazy, undisciplined, or what people today would call a slacker, and (depending on the day of the week and direction of the wind) either too bright to be engaged by the mundane education system (my parents' preferred explanation), or too interested in sports and girls to care about schoolwork.

In today's world, I would have spent hours every week working with therapists, receiving individual and small group behavioral therapy, social therapy, occupational therapy, and physical therapy. I would have had less time to write. I wonder if children today with similar problems don't have time to pursue the interests that could be their saving grace.

I allowed my parents and teachers to think I was all about sports and girls, high on everyone's list of healthy activities for a junior-high-school-age boy. I loved sports and was a reasonably good athlete, playing baseball and basketball and football and, my all-time favorite, stickball, but I was scared of girls, and didn't understand them at all. I found them intimidating and couldn't relax in their presence.

It seems to me that ADD (Attention Deficit Disorder) *should* be called PASE (Paying Attention to Something Else). That's the way it always worked for me, and I saw it repeated in many of the students I taught.

I *was* focused in school, and I *was* paying attention—just to something else (sports, yes, but also especially writing). When I wrote in my head, my concentration was unbreakable. Writing takes discipline, whether you're ten or fifty. In my mind, I would build engaging characters, develop story lines, outline plots, and design intricate settings where my stories would take place. Not only did I create manuscripts in my head, I was able to remember everything until I got home and wrote them down on my trusted yellow pad. No wonder I wasn't paying attention to my teachers—or anyone else!

Today I remain distant when my mind is writing, seemingly having a conversation around a table or at a party, and somehow nodding appropriately, yet not hearing a single word being said.

Under the heading of "great things come from where you least expect them," the same junior-high-school teacher who had taken me to task for writing notes in his class, and kept me after school for detention, helped me snatch victory from the jaws of defeat.

He had promised escalating punishments if the note writing continued, and duly kept me after school when I called his bluff, forcing me to write extra-credit reports. Another miracle. My punishment was being forced to do what I loved to do most—write. The difference was that now I would write to improve my grades ... and, in the process, open the eyes of my parents and teachers in a positive way.

Extra credit got me through high school and into college. I found it could make up for anything: not paying attention, getting poor grades on tests, even missing classes. I sold the "extra-credit solution" to each of my teachers. In class I barely managed a C for class work, homework, participation, and tests, but I always got As in extra credit. So I came home with a report card loaded with Bs, and while my mysterious "potential" was still not perceived as being realized, at last no one had any reason to take me to task, and so left me alone.

I wrote extra-credit reports. I passed. I wrote, I passed, and I was left alone. I wrote, I passed, and I got into college.

If I were the curriculum god of education, I would proclaim that every school offer programs based entirely on extra credit. Take underperforming, disengaged, and discipline-challenged students, and provide them with their own personalized extra-credit curriculum. Call it the Albert Einstein Curriculum. It would start in prekindergarten and continue right through high school. Kids who don't perform in structured classrooms, don't pay attention, or act out—these kids won't be sent to detention, or tested and counseled to death. They'll go to extra credit to write, or sculpt, or learn computer code and create video games.

I'll be there.

Here is why I think children excel in nursery school and under perform soon after entering elementary school. It's because nursery schools know about extra credit, and use it to everyone's advantage. They don't call it extra credit because they understand that education comes in a wide variety of forms and experiences. All children learn: Just sit in on a nursery school class if you don't believe it.

Every time I took one of my kids to nursery school, or picked them up, I wanted to stay.

The Writing Experience

Part 2: The Archaeology of the Mind

One thing I like about digging into the writing experience is how that knowledge peels back layers of the mind and reveals things buried under the surface. You can do the same thing. Here's how to go about it:

First, start by thinking about your mental to-do list for the next week. Your mind expends energy maintaining that information close to your consciousness. Put the list on paper. I'm sure you've done that before. What happens is that as soon as it is written down, you mind lets go, frees up the space, and takes on the ability to work at a deeper level.

Now think about the longer-term projects that similarly take up space and energy. They include things you have put off for a while but still need to get done at some point. *Write them down.* If there's a person you need to talk to about something, write down what you are planning to say: You don't have to give it to the person or ever say it to the person, but the act of writing it all down frees up space and mental energy and allows your creativity to get into the front seat of your consciousness. The end result is that you start to notice a new supply of fresh thoughts entering your mind, without you having to try and make it happen. These are the thoughts that pay dividends in the writing experience every day.

Taking it one step further: Try and think about what you *think about* during the day—and write those thoughts down. Write everything down. It's even good to keep a pad handy and write thoughts down as soon as they come to mind. I find that as I do that, I seem to be peeling back layer after layer of extraneous thoughts, and useful and interesting ideas start to flow freely. Those ideas, over the years, turn into the content for all of your writing.

Just don't let thinking about what you are thinking about become all that you are thinking about.

Some Thoughts on Writing from . . . Richard Lewis

Richard Lewis is the author of two young-adult novels, *The Flame Tree* (2004) and *The Killing Sea* (2007), as well of a number of short stories. Read more about him and his work at his website, richardlewisauthor.com.

My parents were American missionaries to Indonesia, where I was born and raised and still live with my family. No TV as a kid. For entertainment I either read whatever I could get my hands on, or went to the beach. I grew up to be a fit young surfer who did some writing. Now I'm a fat middle-aged writer who does some surfing. Sundays, I go to church and think on questions like "Why would a good God make evil eggplant for man to gag upon?"

I also spend a good deal of my life looking for things, such as my sunglasses, which sometimes are to be found propped up on my head. One time, I took my young son to lunch on my motor scooter. Driving home from the café I had this odd feeling I was forgetting something, which, of course, was my son. He didn't mind, though. The café owner had given him some ice cream. Next day he wanted me to take him out to lunch and forget him all over again.

I grew up in Indonesia without television, so I read from an early age to entertain myself. It only seemed logical to write to entertain myself, as well. When I was six, I wrote a story about a yawn that traveled the world. When I'm seventy-six, I will rewrite the same story.

There are times when I'm writing that I feel as though I'm presenting something true and important about deeper things, perhaps even spiritual things. This is personal, though. I'm a novelist, and one thing a novelist should never do is preach. In a way, the job of a novelist is to examine the tensions and cracks, not the certainties.

Even though I started writing young, and knew in my heart I was a writer, it wasn't until I turned forty that I finally started writing seriously and with discipline. It had taken long detours through various places and jobs and adventures for me to figure out I was most happy when unhappily writing. Filling a void? I write to feed the black dog, keep it sated and snoozing.

I have this suspicion that many writers have a strong dash of the hermit in their personalities. "The Quiet Observer" as my wife calls me. Writing tills the stony ground of my heart, softens it. If I didn't write, I'd be the worst kind of hermit—a grouchy one.

Does writing make you feel more (or less) connected to others? How . . . and, if so, with whom is the connection important?

Ah. The Quiet Observer, having observed, then retreats to his den and creates entire fictional worlds that can be more real to him than the real world outside. This is a danger. In the larger scheme of things, family is more important. I meditate in the mornings, and a key focus of my meditations is my family, to make sure that my day is open to them. Friends, too. In a more practical vein, participating in a community of writers is a good way to not only improve one's writing but to be connected to the real world.

I'm a "gotta write" writer. The black dog isn't happy with anything else. If I had my druthers, I'd rather be a professional mathematician than a writer. A mathematician working at the boundaries discovers something that's never been known before, and his discovery is a unique contribution to a body of truth. A writer? Well, there's nothing new under the sun, no story that hasn't been told before, and told better at that.

My first novel, *The Flame Tree,* tells the story of a friendship between a young American boy, the son of Christian medical missionaries to Java, and a Muslim village boy. It is set against the backdrop of 9/11 and deals in part with Christian-Muslim tensions. In writing the novel, I researched and extended more deeply my understanding of Islam. I was struck at how fundamentally alike the two religions are, starting with yearning for the spiritual and for a spiritual understanding of life, and this is something that has stayed with me.

Let me tell you a story to illustrate what I mean. When I was in Aceh after the 2004 tsunami, helping with relief efforts, I attended the Muslim Eid al-Adha, or Day of Sacrifice, service. Eid al-Adha commemorates Abraham's willingness to sacrifice his son (who is Ishmael in the Islamic tradition). The congregational worship was held on open field. The American government had sent navy ships to the area on a mercy mission, and sitting in the back with me was a US Marine officer. For his benefit, I translated the imam's brief sermon, about Abraham's faith and what it means for us today. The officer's eyes widened. "Good Lord," he said, "I could be back home listening to a sermon from my pastor."

About two-thirds of the way through the first draft of *The Killing Sea*, a story of the 2004 Asian tsunami that draws on my experiences as a relief worker, I hit a brick wall. Not writer's block, for I knew what came next. It was a good, compelling scene. But I couldn't write another word of it. I'd never encountered anything like this. I forced myself to write, each word like gnawing on granite, and eventually the writing became easier.

I put away the finished draft and reread it two days later. As I did so, memories of my time in Aceh and the people I met tumbled through my mind. I had a meltdown. I realized then why I had hit the wall. While writing, I was skating the surface, focusing on the artful crafting of the story and not allowing the deep emotional core of it to bubble up.

Do you have advice for others exploring writing as a means of opening their hearts?

Don't censor yourself. Self-censorship is perhaps the most insidious form of all.

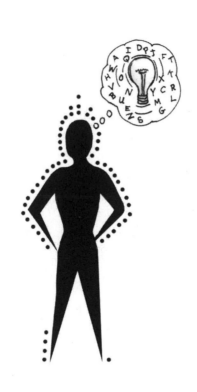

THREE

Wheels

Our language is funny—a fat chance
and a slim chance are the same thing.

—J. GUSTAV WHITE

Growing up in New York, reaching sixteen was as important a milestone for boys as it was for girls. In New York State, in the 1960s, you could get your driver's license at sixteen. You needed to be eighteen to drink, and twenty-one to vote, but sixteen to drive. Today in New York you can vote at eighteen, and not drink until you are twenty-one, so I assume someone decided along the way it takes more responsibility to handle drinking than it does to select the leaders of the country.

I had been thinking about driving since at least the age of ten, and had become increasingly obsessed with the idea for a while, ever since my friends—many of whom were a year older than I was—started getting their licenses. The planning was intricate, combining completing a driver's education course with getting a ride to the motor vehicle bureau to take the written test the exact day of my sixteenth birthday. Once the plan came together, I could take a road test and have my license within thirty days. At sixteen plus thirty days, I traded my two wheels for four.

The license for sixteen-year-olds allowed you to drive during daylight hours, drive to school if you had a car (I didn't), and allowed you to drive to, during, and from work if you had a job (which I made sure I had lined up in advance).

The job consisted of working three nights a week delivering prescriptions for a local pharmacy, using its delivery van.

At sixteen, my days were full, starting with too many hours of high school and participating in organized sports until dark. I played baseball, basketball, and tennis; I was even on the high school bowling team. I loved all of them. When I wasn't practicing, or playing league games on the weekends, I played stickball for hours, stopping only when it became too dark to see. Finally, I spent a couple of hours a week attending religious school.

But three evenings a week, I worked: I drove, I delivered, and I used the solitude driving from delivery to delivery to develop writing skills. It was great.

The job was relatively simple. I entered the store through the back, where there would be a bin full of prescriptions waiting to be delivered. The bin was separated into compartments signifying deliveries going out to different parts of town. I would grab the pile from whichever bin was the most full, make my deliveries, collect monies owed, pocket my tips, and return to the store to repeat the process. If I started at seven in the evening, I could make three complete trips by the time the store closed, around eleven. When the store closed, the owner would usually give me a ride home.

It was being on the road, making deliveries, that was the most exciting part of the job. I would drive that van all over town, mostly delivering prescriptions to elderly people or to those stuck at home because of a lack of transportation, or because they had too many kids to watch. My rampant imagination made it possible for me to find a wonderful story behind every single delivery. Here, let me give you an example:

The Quiet House

The building was huge, taking up an entire city block, and it was set back what had to be at least one hundred feet from the sidewalk. It was by far the biggest apartment building in town. From inside the building you could see that the four sides of the building surrounded a protected courtyard where the residents could spend a nice quiet afternoon on a sunny day. I learned later that the apartment house had been built after World War II to help spur the local economy and provide jobs for returning soldiers.

The outer shell of the building was brick—not the elegant red brick that catches your eye, but yellow brick, or possibly white brick that had turned yellow over the years. The windows were small and evenly spaced over the exterior, giving you the feeling that the building could have been a factory, or a prison, or a mental institution for that matter, but it was just a huge apartment building. There were only a few large trees scattered on the vast expanse of neatly trimmed lawn, and equally few colorful flower gardens sitting close to the building itself, carefully designed and very well taken care of.

I could take all of this in, even on a dark night, because every part of the exterior of the building was extremely well lit. The overall effect was a building that stood without pride, but also without shame, utilitarian, doing what it was meant to do, and with a sense that it was going to continue to do its job far into the future.

I was buzzed in, and I opened the door.

The hallways were endless and the deafening silence was the color of coal dust. The wall-to-wall carpet was hard and smooth enough to navigate a wheelchair, but padded enough to be sure I didn't disturb the silence. I found a wide stairway directly to my left that would take me to the third floor, and didn't bother looking for an elevator. Taking the stairs two steps at a time on the springy legs of a sixteen-year-old athlete, I entered the third floor in a few seconds, and came out directly across from apartment thirty-nine. I knew I had a ways to go before reaching my destination at the other end of the hallway and looked down a hallway so long, and so poorly lit in comparison to the brightness outside, that I wasn't even sure I could see the other end.

As I walked down the hall, my senses slowly got accustomed to the silence, and sounds began to creep in. It was the normal sounds a building makes, I suppose, heat or air conditioning moving through ducts, somewhere a chair scraping on the floor, and maybe, in the far distance a television or radio playing. In the middle of winter, at seven-thirty in the evening, I would have expected to hear a television blaring behind every door.

I reached number thirty-one. I knocked and was told to enter.

She sat in a high-backed armchair directly across the room from the open door, facing the door, looking up at me when I entered with no discernable expression on her face, or certainly one that was unreadable to me. There was a floor lamp on one side of her chair and I recognized the oxygen tank standing upright on the opposite side. The room was neat but dusty. I took in, but didn't recognize the medical machine that took up a good deal of the wall behind her, the one from which the tubes attached to her body, and to the oxygen tank emerged. I handed her the small bag of medication and her hand, dry as stone, and as thin as onion paper, rested for a split second against mine. She asked me quietly to get her a glass of water as she removed her pills from the bag and opened the container.

Returning from the sink, I waited a minute while she took her pill, my mind running in all different directions and hoping she didn't throw all of the pills in the bottle into her mouth and swallow them down with a quick swig of water. She handed me the glass and for just a second I thought she was going to say something, maybe ask for something, maybe tell me something I wouldn't want to hear. But she didn't utter a word, and I returned the glass to the sink. She called me over one more time and slipped a quarter into my palm, and I thanked her and left the apartment. I had probably been there no more than a couple of minutes.

As I walked down the hallway, growing more accustomed to the building every second, additional sounds came to me and I recognized, or imagined, that they had nothing to do with heat or air conditioning or the normal sounds of an apartment house. It was her machine I could hear in the background, louder now than even when I was inside her apartment. Soon I could hear that same machine behind every door I passed in that endless hallway. I became convinced that those machines were keeping the residents of the apartment building alive, and I realized in a moment of true clarity that they couldn't play their televisions or the radios without fear of blowing a fuse and with it, life. The further I walked the more sensitive I became and the louder the machines whirred in my ears, there was no longer one machine behind every door, but now it was everywhere. It was all consuming.

I worked myself up pretty good by the time I reached the double doors that would take me out of the building. I moved across the wide cement path toward the van as I was leaving, realizing it had been only a few minutes earlier when I had come to make my delivery.

As I started to pull away, I looked through my rearview mirror and saw the building shudder once, then a second time, through the cold night fumes of my exhaust, and I matched it with one of my own that shook my entire body.

This was only the beginning. I could—and couldn't—wait to come back.

The End

Already Completed In My Mind

The first thing I did every night when I arrived home after work was to grab a pad, kept now in a bedside drawer rather than under the covers, and sit at my desk recording my stories for posterity. I paid careful attention to the details of each and every encounter, spending time thinking about the setting and the characters. The plots always seemed to build themselves. I passed interesting people all over town, who (I was sure) would be thrilled with the characters I had made them into, and the exciting lives I'd created for them. I made them the heroes and villains in my books. Some were young with lives just getting started, and other lives were drawing to a close. None of their lives were boring.

The nights I worked empowered me to write, but not always creatively. If I had a paper due for school—and, yes, I continued to write extra-credit reports all through high school and college—riding around in that van gave me the time I needed to organize the paper, and prepare my words in advance, so I could simply add research and record it on paper when I arrived home.

I have never sat down, with pad or paper, or at a typewriter, or facing my computer for that matter, without having the bulk of whatever I was working on, a story or poem, a school report or term paper, already completed in my mind. I was recording what I had already written—in the van, or standing in the outfield, or while daydreaming my way through chemistry.

The Writing Experience

Part 3: There's More than One Way to Find a Story

I have recognized over the years that my story lines materialize from a host of different sources, and I try to develop useful techniques (they work really well for me) to be sure I have a constant stream of exciting new story lines of my own. In addition, when working with other writers, or teaching writing to children, I have seen these tools being useful to the writer when integrated with his or her own writing habits.

In this chapter, the story I wrote was initiated by a setting: the apartment house. That was what grabbed my atten-

A Character Library

tion first, and in enlarging on the setting of the apartment, the woman who lived there and her machine came to life. The building, as the setting, was the star of the story, and everything started there. So one thing I do is to develop my own library of settings where future stories might take place.

You drive or walk by multiple locations every day that are just waiting to be brought to life in the pages of your next book. Develop your own setting library. Try to add one setting to your library weekly, and every few months be sure to go back and read through them—continuing to improve their descriptions and letting them settle comfortably in your mind. Over time, each setting in your library will grow richer with possibility, and one day you will be working on a book and one of those settings will jump out at you as the perfect place for that book to be situated. In addition, reading through your settings library provides inspiration just when you think you have run out of ideas.

Another way to build content it is to give a character the lead and let him or her show you where a story needs to go. Again, you see multiple character opportunities every day in your travels. Build a character library of people you see daily, the guy sitting on the porch wondering if he'll ever find another job, and the woman cleaning your house who will find out in a few hours she has won the lottery. Again, once every few months, review your characters, continue to refine each one a little bit, add depth to their personalities, and let them become your imaginary friends. Soon, as you spend more and more time together, you'll find they are telling you their own stories.

When you think about writing, keep in mind that it doesn't matter if you start with a plot, a setting, or a character. In the end, the story fills out to include all the elements you need for success.

An additional bonus of this exercise is that it helps fight writer's block. When my mind is blank and refusing to cooperate, I go back to creating a single character, or elaborating on a setting—completely outside of a plot or other structure. I've found this exercise has gotten me past whatever was holding me back, and soon I am in the flow of my next project.

FOUR

Wordsworth, Keats, Byron, and Shelley

If my doctor told me I had only six minutes to live,
I wouldn't brood. I'd type a little faster.

—ISAAC ASIMOV

e all know the saying: "Give a man a fish and he'll eat for a day, teach a man to fish and he will eat for a lifetime," . . . but give a fish to one of the great Romantic poets of the late 1800s and early 1900s and he will cry in uncontrollable joy at the generosity of the gift, sit down at his desk and write in five hundred words or less how the fish you gave him was the biggest, the bravest, the strongest, and the most beautiful fish ever to roam the seven seas. After that, he will bemoan in thousands upon thousands of words how he is poor, starving to death, wilting away, just a shadow of his former self, all while a bountiful meal of Flounder Florentine lies within arms reach, but untouchable as he could never bring himself to eat such a wondrous gift.

It was during my sophomore year in college, in my first elective course, that I met the Romantic poets; they captured my heart and imagination. It was the first time in school—almost fourteen years' worth of school—when I can honestly say I looked forward to

Mr. Romantic Poet

being in the classroom every day, to spending time doing assignments carefully and thoughtfully, and to paying attention to the teacher, who was *finally* speaking my language.

The poems we read in class—"The Rime of the Ancient Mariner," "Ode to the West Wind," "Don Juan," and "Ode on a Grecian Urn," among others—and those we read on our own—were full of love, and lust, and always self-denial, as were the poets who wrote them. They needed to create pain, to live pain, to immerse themselves in pain, in order to write the pain and bring pleasure to others.

There have been times when I have been writing and experienced some of what the Romantic poets went through in the name of art. Times when I have been bursting with the need to write, but words wouldn't come . . . or times when I have been bursting with the need to write, and only the wrong words would come . . . and times when I have been bursting with words, but had nothing to say.

I have spontaneously fallen in love with ideas, and with people who were out of my reach, and I have allowed myself to wallow in the wanting of the impossible. Sometimes, when I'm in love, the words flow easily and it feels wonderful, and sometimes they don't flow at all and I feel miserable.

While writing this book I have been called by inhabitants of other books who want me to pay attention to them. Marcellina is a character in a mystery I started a while ago and put aside, I told myself, until this book was finished. This woman just won't leave me alone! She isn't interested in waiting until I am ready to pay attention to her. And there is Michael Mast, the main character in a novel on which I am working . . . I started the novel a few years ago and reached a point where Michael stopped talking to me, stopped telling me where he was going or what he was thinking. Wouldn't you know that as soon as I begin another project, he decides he is ready to talk to me?

I set mental magnets to influence what my mind pays attention to, but I have little control over when it will deliver the goods. Sometimes I give myself something to think about and later in the day the answer pops out; other times it's weeks or months later when the response finally comes. But when it does, whether in five minutes or five months, the call is strong, bringing with it an overwhelming temptation to change direction. I suspect you've felt that way sometimes, too.

Fortunately for me (and my publisher!) the need to stay with this project has won out, and I hope Marcellina and Michael are waiting for me, calling me as strongly as they are now, when I am ready to get back to them. There are always many books going on in my head at the same time—books, poems, songs, articles and notes that need to be written; I think that's probably true for most creative people. Keeping it in some kind of balance is a major challenge.

The Romantic poets made an art of delayed gratification, whether real or imagined. They needed to cry out for the fulfillment they imagined was waiting around the next corner. Unrequited love was the cornerstone of their writing.

Sometimes I get to feeling that I've met each of them in person, possibly in some previous life. One reason for this sense of familiarity, no doubt, is that their poems are my note writing—only pumped up on steroids.

I bet that Wordsworth, Keats, Shelley, Byron, and the rest spent as much time in detention in high school as I did, probably running circles around me writing extra-credit reports to pass their courses.

I see one of them sitting in class by the window on a sunny spring day, watching mesmerized as a beautiful girl walks by, one that he had never seen, and would never see again. From the time she enters his vision until she disappears isn't more than ten seconds, yet in that short amount of time he falls head over heels in lust with her and vows eternal love.

Immediately he turns to his writing pad and begins to write clever, funny, witty, sensual notes that he'll hand to her through the window the next time she walks by. The note writing goes on for weeks and fills page after page in his notebooks, until he admits to himself the foregone conclusion that she isn't going to ever pass his way again.

Of course, being a romantic poet-in-training, this is a good thing, it's what he lives for; he takes his beautiful, warm, funny, and lustful notes and translates them into poems. His pain, and the testimony of his undying love, are recorded for posterity.

My enthusiasm for the Romantic poets was enhanced by the fact that in my sophomore year in college I had my first poem published.

Womb with a View

To be, to see
I want to be,
From restraining walls
Soon set free
This once large world
Containing me
No Longer Whirled
Stale ecstasy
I want to be
Free
To be
Me.

The publication of "Womb with a View" grew out of the experience of sharing my words with other people for the first time. I had no choice. Right from day one, in class each week, students read assignments aloud to the class, followed by a full class critique of the writing. Once the reading was complete, the author handed out copies to each student in the class and the discussion began. It was often brutal, and frequently writing was overanalyzed by students hell-bent on making a lasting impression on the professor. The professor, however, was masterful at maintaining a positive direction, and the safety net was that each student was aware that the day was coming when her or his work would be critiqued, and payback, as they say, could be a bitch.

Having my work read and critiqued by my professor and classmates was eye-opening. I found my fear that every word I wrote could be a door to my soul was unfounded. I am not what I write . . . at least, most of the time I'm not.

I learned that I was a writer with some promise. This provided a confidence boost that encouraged me to continue writing and improved my overall college experience. I still participated in sports, and hung out with jocks, but whereas in the past my entire social life revolved around sports, I now had another social outlet: hanging out with other writers.

Writing expanded my world. Education took on new meaning, suddenly earning my respect. It was more than a great professor and a great class that captured my heart: The college environment, with its free flow of ideas and its emphasis on learning over teaching, was a good fit for my learning style.

I enrolled in a weekend course in college; the professor was Isaac Asimov. He talked about the twentieth century, all one hundred years of the twentieth century, and it was only the sixties. He talked about the 1980s, still twenty years away, as easily and with as much detail as he talked about the 1940s. He had seen it all, and each day was as clear to him as any other. He understood the threads that were woven through all hundred years, while I still looked at world wars, the Depression, women's lib, black power, the Vietnam War, and so on, as unique incidents. He showed me a century dominated by unrest and by the superego of underdog groups fighting to find their voice, fighting to be heard by everyone else.

It is similar to the way events unfold in life, day-to-day happenings seeming unrelated. But looking back, years in the future, you see the flow in how you got from one place to another, and you understand why it caught your attention.

When you have recorded your life in the form of notes, poems and stories, the "looking back" experience is richer. I started note writing in elementary school, and never stopped. When I read things I wrote in the past, the content is enlightening and the words are often frightening.

Today I have a far greater appreciation of how important it is to pay attention to not only what you say, but also to how the words sound as they roll off your tongue.

In a poem, every word draws a picture of its own for the reader. It could be said that this is true in anything you write, and it is. I do believe, though, that it's essential in poetry.

The reality is that writing poetry helps improve your prose. The focus on succinct thoughts, translated to a page in a few dynamic, well-chosen words, can make tremendous improvements in your writing.

Although the subject matter is different, even my business writing has been influenced by poetry. In both poetry and business writing, extra words are a nuisance.

The One Minute Manager, likely the shortest serious business book ever written, is a prime example of taking this idea to an extreme. The book is wildly successful, a best seller. Today, when so much attention is focused on the speed of the Internet, it is mandatory for writers to say what they need to say quickly, to get to the point.

After college I taught elementary school, fourth and fifth grades, all subjects. I was acutely aware that individual children had different learning styles, and tried to modify my classroom accordingly, to accommodate a wide range of children. It wasn't easy, and I wasn't always successful, but placing the responsibility on myself to maintain a classroom environment designed to meet the needs of each child had positive results.

I stayed after school nearly every day to write, laughingly calling it detention, and at least a few of the children in the class hung out with me.

They were probably hoping to meet the Romantic poets.

The Writing Experience

Part 4: Stop, Look, and Listen

What I mostly learned from my professor was to stop, look, and listen. He taught us that when something catches your attention as you read, for whatever reason, stop and try to understand what it is that grabbed you, look at the words and phrases and see if you find something special about them. Read them aloud and listen to how the words flow. In other words, see if they caught your eye for a reason—or multiple reasons—that you can articulate. Assume that the writer stopped you on purpose: If you understand why, it will help you get a better feel for the work you are reading.

He suggested that when we are writing, we could improve our work by taking a similar approach by using others to help us better understand how readers are affected by our words. In class, we would not only read our assignments out loud to the rest of the class, for constructive criticism, but we would also read each other's work out loud and give the author a chance to hear his or her words read by a different voice.

Always read at least part of what you write out loud, even if only to yourself. It is important to read out loud because as you write you are already reading the words silently, you know how they sound to your mind, but not always to your ears. Reading them again, out loud, creates a new sense of how your words flow and work together. Listen to your own voice and pay attention to things that make you pause, or bring you to a full stop in your writing. Did you stop because a phrase caught your imagination, or because it was awkward and didn't flow comfortably? Be aware of places your mind wants to skip over and see if you need to eliminate it—or add something to get your readers' attention and slow them down.

Some people believe that only poems and songs are designed to be

"listened" to, but in fact, it is valuable to read aloud some or all of everything you write. You have a voice and you will hear it more clearly when you follow this practice. In addition, make a practice of having others, friends and family, read your work out loud to you. As they read, pay attention to where they hesitate, or stumble across words and phrases, and where words just roll off their tongue. Listen for places where you have written phrases in such a way as to speed up the way they read, and be equally aware where your words slow them down.

You have power, and it is important to understand it and use it to your advantage.

Whatever effect your words have in others' voices is neither good nor bad; words are simply tools. As a writer, be aware that you can control the pace of your readers: Slow them down when you want to, and speed them up when you are taking them down a path where you want to catch them by surprise at the end. When the reading pace speeds up, the reader lets her guard down; when you slow the reader down, her guard starts to work overtime. It is similar to the way producers use music in the movies and on television to control your emotional readiness for the coming action.

Stop, look, and listen, and improve the quality of your writing dramatically.

FIVE

The Circus Comes to Town

A writer is someone who is enormously taken
by things anyone else would walk by.

—JAMES DICKEY

I was one year out of college and heading to an interview for a teaching job, a career for which I had not taken a single course in college.

I was interested in teaching primarily because it gave me a deferment from the draft and would keep me out of Vietnam. Since there was a shortage of teachers at the time, school districts were hiring college graduates without teaching degrees to fill vacancies. As an added bonus, after teaching for one year in New York, you were granted a lifetime teaching certificate waiving all educational requirements, including student teaching.

The town I was looking for was Somers, New York, located in northern Westchester County, an hour north of New York City. The area in 1969 was scarcely populated, with houses scattered randomly on the countryside between working farms and acres of forest, with no shopping malls or centralized cityscape or flashing neon lights to interrupt the beauty.

Following pre-Mapquest handwritten directions, and paying

attention because there was no such thing as a GPS to tell me when to turn, I finally reached Route 202. Making a left turn, I slowed almost to a crawl, noticing two things.

The first was a tall granite pillar that rose fifty feet or more in the air, starting from the grass in the triangle of lawn marking the center of the intersection, and on top of which stood . . . what else, but a metal elephant.

The second was a three-story red brick building off to the right side of the intersection, with a hand-painted sign on the façade proclaiming it to be the Elephant Hotel. *What have I gotten myself into?* I wondered, with only half a smile, as I continued down the road to my destination. It was a school building that looked exactly like what you would expect: red stone, old, two stories high, and set back on a huge expanse of lawn, with a broad entrance centered on the building. On one side of the fifteen-foot-wide entrance walkway was a very old, very large tree, and on the other side, a tall flagpole, complete with flag. The grounds were quiet.

Inside was another story. There was hustle and bustle everywhere, with students and teachers making their way between classrooms. Years later I remembered that day when, as a member of the faculty, I saw a group of children running in the hall. Just as I was about to let them know in no uncertain terms that they shouldn't be running in the hall, their teacher, a great friend of mine, rounded the corner, looked up at me and exclaimed, "How great is it that they're so excited to be going to the library?"

Lesson learned.

I soon became excited about the possibility of working in that environment. Leaving town, I slowed the car once more as I passed the two landmarks: The Elephant Hotel, and the elephant itself staring down on me. I had been too nervous to ask anyone I met about the elephant—why is it that you always think of the really important questions after the interview is long over?

I didn't give it another thought, until as luck would have it, I got the job and a month later had moved into town, ready to start my career. I showed up the day before Labor Day for new-teacher orientation, and the first question I asked was, "What's with the elephant?" Right? Wrong. Something happens when you start a new job, and I was so focused on meeting new people, getting my classroom ready for the coming school year, taking part in faculty meetings, and getting to know the children in my class, that months went by and I still hadn't asked about the elephant. In fact, by now I drove by it two or three times a day without giving it a glance or a second thought.

But eventually all questions find their way to answers, and everything I wanted to know about the elephant came to light when I was sitting in the faculty lunchroom one day and overheard a group of teachers talking about Old Bet.

Here is the story of Old Bet:

Old Bet was the second elephant ever brought into the United States, arriving in Boston in 1804, and acquired by Hachaliah Bailey of Somers, New York, soon thereafter. By 1808, Hachaliah Bailey had sold off shares in his elephant to two other partners for $1,200 each.

In 1825 Bailey's three-story brick "Elephant Hotel" was completed in Somers with a granite pillar supporting a statue of an elephant.

Step forward with me a couple of years. I was comfortable with my job, the curriculum, and the faculty and administration, and I was branching out in creative directions as a teacher. The school district encouraged teachers to bring new ideas into the classroom, and we had actually established one of the first open schools in the area, with a new building designed to create flexible classroom spaces. (One year I taught math by building and racing go-carts around the perimeter of the school, helping children learn everything from building blueprints to understanding how weight and wheel size and a curving track all ultimately affect speed.)

As busy as I was teaching twenty-five nine- and ten-year-old children, during this time I never stopped writing. There have been few times when I have, but for the most part the first few years I taught I limited myself to writing poems and songs, which required a shorter attention span, and were more useful in the classroom.

My fourth year teaching, I had a class that really inspired me: children who were exciting to work with, curious, mature, and ready to try anything that sounded like fun. The classroom became amazingly collaborative. I was caught up in the adventure, and it was somehow not at all surprising when, out of nowhere, came the idea for a musical.

That's right: We would write and perform a musical. I had never attempted it before, either alone or with a class. Working together we would create it, soup to nuts, and at the end of the year perform it for the entire school. It is a truly wonderful thing that youth (both mine and the children's) had no idea of its limitations.

The school year progressed and the project grew geometrically, sometimes under control and at other times totally out of control. As the performance date neared it expanded and consumed almost all of the human resources in the school. And the result was truly phenomenal. My first musical, created in collaboration with twenty-five nine- and ten-year-old children, ranks as one of the most incredible experiences of my life. I was amazed at how children, administration, faculty, and aides worked side-by-side bringing it to fruition, but I get ahead of myself here.

After weeks of thought, give and take, and planning, the brain trust that was our class agreed on the only possible theme for our musical: the elephant, the circus, Hachaliah Bailey, and all the rest that goes with it. The first song we wrote was titled "It's Hard to Make an Elephant Smile," and when that song was finished and I heard the class sing it with their music teacher, I knew the musical was really going to happen.

We wrote the script and sang the songs in class, editing as we went along. The story almost wrote itself, but the creativity that turned it into a performance was hard work.

I had no idea how to write music when we started this project and I'm still not sure I do, although I have written two more since that first one, and am working on another that I hope to complete this year. I can play basic chords on the guitar, and I have a voice that can empty a room faster than a snake coming at you; that was enough to get us where we needed to go—at least until the music teacher was able to take over! We wrote lyrics together and I tried to find chords on the guitar that went along with them. If I couldn't find the right chords we would try to sing the song to the music

On My Guitar

teacher, but usually ended up showing him the words while I (mercifully, he pointed out) limited myself to humming the tune.

To give you an idea of the scope of the project, let me share a bit of the title song for the show, simply called "Hachaliah," and elaborate on how we built the song into an opening production number.

Hachaliah

Hachaliah Bailey, a man of ideas
Always on the go,
Full of surprises,
He opened our eyes
To the world's greatest show
He brought us the star of the show
This town started to grow
And it hasn't
Stopped growing yet
That's why we remember
Hachaliah Bailey
And we'll never forget
Old Bet
That's why we remember
Hachaliah Bailey
And we'll never forget
Old Bet.

It was important to the class (well, for me more than for the children) that our musical get off to a really "big" start and capture the audience's attention right out of the gate. Growing up, I was a huge fan of the really big musicals like *Oklahoma* and *West Side Story*. I love musicals because they are a true celebration of life. To get our musical, *Ol' Bet*, off to the kind of start we wanted, the children went from one end of Somers to the other taking pictures of the old and the new, showing how the town was changing, trying to create, with the art teacher's help, a visual feel for what Somers looked like both in the early 1800s (some parts of town had hardly changed at all, including an old still-operational covered bridge) and in the 1970s.

The best photographs were chosen and turned into a slide presentation. When the show opened, the lights went down, the title song was sung by the children, accompanied by the music teacher, and the audience was treated to a celebration of the town of Somers, old and new, all presented in slides projected onto a big screen.

The audience loved seeing how dramatically the town had changed over the years, and immediately got totally engaged in the show. The slide presentation was repeated at the end.

To this day I have never been involved in a project that brought so many people together over such a long period of time for a singular purpose. There was a teacher's aide I worked with who was an amazing seamstress. She designed the costumes, creating an elephant costume that was worn by two children, one in front and the other taking up the rear. Watching these kids in the elephant costume pout and slump and finally dance with glee during the singing of "It's Hard to Make an Elephant Smile," was another great moment in the show.

The art teacher worked with the kids to make scenery, and the music teacher turned the class into an incredible chorus, with outstanding soloists. Many parents gave countless hours helping in every way possible. Even the principal had a role in the show, as Hachaliah himself. It was at this time, creating this musical, where I first experienced the power of collaboration, and to this day it influences every project I undertake.

Open Your Heart with Writing

The Writing Experience

Part 5: Jacks or Better to Open

In poker, the conventional wisdom is that you shouldn't open a hand unless you have jacks or better — jacks, queens, kings, or aces. In other words, start with a strong hand. It works that way in writing, too. Sometimes I ask myself why I write notes, songs, essays, articles, stories, novels, and musicals, all in a random way, instead of picking one area and sticking to it, developing my skills in greater depth, and maybe finding an audience.

Part of the reason is that I don't have a choice. It sounds silly to say that, even to me, and I'm the one saying it. Why not just sit down and say, *okay, Neil, write an article?* There is no reason I can't do that. The problem is that when I sit down to write that article, a song comes out instead. I can focus on the article, and probably even get it done, but at the end of the day the song isn't going to leave me alone until it is done also.

So what does that have to do with you, and how does knowing that help you to become a better writer?

The idea of "Jacks or Better to Open" means having a basic set of skills or information you need to participate in the game. When the game is writing, Jacks or Better to Open refers to the ability to create a scene, develop a character, and create a plot line. No matter what you are writing, these skills are mandatory.

Every song has a least one character you want your audience to take an interest in. Something happens to that character—he gets hurt in love, or she takes part in building the Erie Canal—and the song takes place somewhere, has its own setting. These are the basic writing elements and you need them to play the game, even to write notes.

• 48 •

Pay attention to these elements in everything you write. In that way, no matter *what* you write, you use the process to become a better writer. In fact, varying what you write creates opportunities to improve your skills.

When writing a note, or a song, or a short poem, you have to develop each element using few words, an ability that comes in handy even when you move on to writing your novel.

At work, I frequently need to distill the core elements of my business to very few words—something called "the elevator pitch"—in order to capture the attention of potential customers and/or investors. (Don't think that writers escape from the elevator pitch: If you can't summarize your book in the moments it takes you to ride from the first to the eighth floor, you're not ready for prime time. It's what you use in your query and cover letters. Don't underestimate its importance.)

Once I use the elevator pitch to get people's attention, I have the opportunity to tell them the whole story, down to the smallest detail. My elevator pitches are usually successful because I use my note writing, poem writing, and songwriting skills to make the point quickly and accurately.

My business plans are equally successful when I can rely on those skills along with others I build developing longer works like novels, musicals, or this book, whose category I would refer to as creative nonfiction.

To become a better writer, worry less about the form of writing you undertake, and more about doing a great job developing the basic elements of your product. Always have Jacks or Better to Open.

SIX

Nota Bene—
Note Well

The difference between the right word and the almost right word
is the difference between lightning and a lightning bug.

—MARK TWAIN

It wasn't possible to come of age in the sixties and seventies without feeling the music flow through your veins—filling your head every waking moment.

There was folk music, and rock and roll, of course—the Beatles, the Stones, the Dead, and Zeppelin are still popular forty years later. There was Motown (the Times performed at my high school prom in 1964), and love songs (think the Righteous Brothers), and protest songs from Peter, Paul and Mary, and Bob Dylan, and dance tunes, and show songs, and story songs like Arlo Guthrie's "Alice's Restaurant."

But to me there were only two ways to differentiate music: music where you could hear and understand the lyrics and music where you couldn't. Guess which type I loved? For me, it's always about the words.

I wanted to write like Dylan, or Smokey Robinson, or any of the others, or have the satisfaction of singing with the Rolling Stones.

Although Dylan's voice itself was grating, his sense of timing and intricate cadences made it impossible to even sing many of his songs, let alone pick them on the guitar. Today I no longer want to be Bob Dylan. But I'd sure like to write songs with as much impact as those he writes, or write songs that go straight to the heart like Smokey Robinson's, or songs that speak to an entire generation, like those of the Beatles.

The Beatles introduced an entire generation to Mary Jane and to meditation, making us seriously consider alternative lifestyles. The Stones drove our emotions with pure power. It was still the early days of rock and roll, but forty years later, it is still the music of choice for my children.

My children and their friends, all in their twenties, were visiting on a recent weekend complaining how the music of their generation hasn't reached the level of the sixties and seventies, when they think it all started. We talked about post-seventies genres, like disco, reggae, and rap. "Each of those is a watered-down variation on rock and roll, and not nearly as powerful as the original," was the conclusion. Something needs to come along to replace it once and for all. But that won't happen until the baby-boomer generation is long gone.

I spent hours when I was in my twenties picking out songs on the guitar. Sometimes I would learn songs written by others and play them until they were permanently etched in my memory. I would know the words, but when I sang, each song ended up having some verses changed or totally rewritten, frequently as a spoof, but sometimes in all seriousness. The feelings each song generated were what turned me on. I feel the love or anger in songs as if it were a core part of my existence.

So I continue to be a copycat, to use others to improve my own writing. It's not stealing: It's learning.

As you know, I have always taken other writers' stories and, as writing exercises, added my own characters to them, or taken well-drawn-out characters and written a new story around them, or a new ending, and so on. So of course I took Dylan, and the Beatles, and the Stones, and the Grateful Dead, and other songwriters' materials and wrote new stanzas as I pleased; often, I am sure, to the detriment of the song.

> So how many times should a man
>   walk alone
> In a place where he never has been?
> And how many times should he sleep
>   on the street
> Passing eyes judging his sins?
> The answer my friend
> Is blowing in the wind . . .

Is it all an exercise in redundancy, a copycat mentality? No: It's more important than that. I undertake these exercises because they hone my writing skills and build my confidence as a writer. When it comes down to it, I hope that my own writing is fresh and original. My ability to create structure around characters, or plot, or setting, has improved, though, by practicing using the works of writers I admire and enjoy reading.

It is easy to isolate a single piece of the writing process when the other pieces are in place—create a character to add to an existing story, or add a stanza to an existing song—but later, when you write on your own, you still have to put it all together successfully.

Great songwriters have always been a powerful force in society, because they depict the pulse of the society and have a huge audience. The songwriters of the sixties and seventies had a powerful effect on how people thought about the Vietnam War, ultimately influencing policy at the highest levels.

Politicians should pay attention to what children listen to on their iPods . . .

I had my first collaborative writing experience when I started to write songs in college, even before *Ol' Bet*. One of the attractions of learning to play guitar, and I use this term loosely, and sing other people's songs, was that I could sit down with friends and jam to a common denominator. In addition, we would share songs we had written and play those, getting a good feel for the quality of what we had written. A few times I wrote songs that were performed by professional singers at local venues.

Prior to songwriting, my writing was a solitary avocation. Possibly I wanted to protect my thoughts, or was scared to share them. Maybe the primary reason writing is solitary, though, is that I can't write on demand and I never know when I am actually going to *have to* sit down and write. My brain has a mind of its own and makes me wait until it is ready to say something before it delivers words to my consciousness. Of course there are things I do to nudge it along, trick it, catch it unawares, make it think it is ready before it actually is, but none of those methods are reliable, and, at the end of the day words come out when they are good and ready, whether I am or not.

Songwriting presents opportunities for collaboration because the words and the music don't have to be created at the same time. I have written lyrics for other songwriters' music, and their music often spurred lyrics. Songwriting teams have been a fact of life for as long as I can remember, especially on Broadway. Many musicals were written by great teams such a Rodgers and Hammerstein, Andrew Lloyd Webber and Charles Hart, Jule Styne and Stephen Sondheim, Elton John and Tim Rice, and others.

In the course of my own collaborative songwriting, I often wonder which comes first, the lyrics or the tune, the words or the music.

I've asked other writers how their process works and for some the lyrics come first, for others the music inspires them to write words, and a large group has told me it varies from song to song and they have written both ways.

Sometimes I put a tune to a poem I have written, and other times I write lyrics for a tune I pick out on the guitar. Neither way seems consistently more effective than the other. When I write musicals, however, there's a progression I always follow.

First comes the plot of the musical, followed by character development, then the lyrics, and finally the music. It is a clear progression, but most of the time once the music is in place, I go back to rewrite the lyrics, usually dramatically improving the song.

Even though I play few chords on the guitar, and infrequently surprise myself by carrying a tune in my dreadful voice, I do not fool myself into thinking my talent lies anywhere beyond writing lyrics. I have written three full musicals and hundreds of songs, a few performed publicly to small local groups, and it is an incredibly rewarding experience.

I think the major reason I haven't tried to publish my songs, or musicals, is because I don't do the music part. But I love songwriting! It has brought the world closer, been something powerful to share with others, and I have great plans to take my musicals to the next level in retirement.

The one biggest reason I love songwriting is that it takes my favorite junior high school and high school pastime—note writing—to another level. Songs take simple ideas and repeat them over and over to be sure the listener gets the point, then add explanation around that major point, creating variation on the theme, but not enough variation to give the listener a sense that something other than the chorus matters.

Here's an example of my note writing put to music.

Waiting
Waiting for the moment
You return
The blue to the darkened sky
The calm to the earth

I've carried yesterday
Through all the days
And months and years,
Now it sits beside me endlessly
Waiting through my tears

Waiting
Waiting for the moment
You return
The blue to the darkened sky
The calm to the earth

So I'm reaching now
Toward the sky
To push the clouds aside
Only together
Can we reach so high
Alone it looks so far

Waiting
Waiting for the moment
You return
The blue to the darkened sky
The calm to the earth.

Lyrics, without music, aren't really a song; maybe they're just a poem. So put some music to it and sing the words above however you would like; turn it from a poem into your own song. Use lyrics as your story line, and music to develop emotions. The lyrics in the above song could create feelings of hopelessness or hopefulness. The tune will help you experience feelings the writer wanted to convey.

It's also important to read lyrics before you listen to a song, so when you listen to it you can see if you get the emotions *right*. With the lyrics already in your head, the music becomes more top-of-mind. Rarely do words alone convey the power and meaning or the emotion of the songwriter.

The opposite is also frequently true. Listen to a song with the lyrics stripped out (elevator music, for example), and try to picture the lyrics in your mind. When you hear the entire song, see how on target you were.

A great example of this is the songs used for the James Bond 007 movies. The lyrics, when you read them, are fairly nondescript, but the music makes them downright chilling. Sitting in the movies, the music plays me like a puppeteer, just as it does the rest of the audience, making us squirm in our seats on demand, letting us sit back and relax for a moment, then pulling us right back to the edge of our chairs. It is the combination of the music and on-screen action that overpowers the script, and our senses, rendering the script almost meaningless.

Songwriting is both very difficult and very fulfilling. I migrate more naturally to writing musicals because I am drawn to stories, to weaving plots, and to building characters; once all that is in place, I can integrate the power of music and lyrics.

Thinking about how the spontaneous overflow of powerful emotion works in the songwriting process is intriguing. Powerful emotions come at you from very different places. One is where lyrics or a poem are powerful enough to motivate you to put them to music, another where music has screamed out to you write lyrics that do it justice.

A songwriter once told me that the most powerful emotion of all for the songwriter is simply when you are so struck by an event or a moment in time that you cannot control your need to burst into song. Powerful emotion indeed, recollected in peaceful tranquility . . . or not.

The Writing Experience

Part 6: Note Well

I am stuck with thoughts of sticky notes floating around in my head. Wouldn't it be wonderful if they came in different sizes? The note-size is obvious, but let's add song-size, essay-size, novel-size, and encyclopedia-size sticky notes. All writing is a short note, or string of short notes attached by an umbilical cord known as the writer's personality.

So let's take notes to songwriting. Take a song you know, write each stanza for that song on its own sticky note. Now write your own stanza on a separate note and add it to the pile. Mix them together and sing the song with your stanza wherever it happened to come out. Sing it for others and see your stanza accepted as a part of the song.

Now write a set of your own lyrics on sticky notes and sing them to different tunes. Start with a fast beat, move on to something slow, and even try a calypso beat. Each change in rhythm and beat recreates the song. I used to have a keyboard that could be set to create different background beats and base lines, allowing me to punch out a melody line on the keyboard. It was great fun to play melodies for hours against all of these different backgrounds.

Finally, take a CD—of music only—and on notes write whatever comes into your head for lyrics to the music you are listening to. It makes no difference if you are listening to classical, country and western, or rock and roll, and don't try to make your lyrics fit the style of the music. Just write out what your heart tells you to.

You will surprise yourself with how good the results are as you become . . . a songwriter!

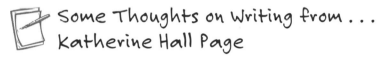

Some Thoughts on Writing from . . . Katherine Hall Page

Katherine Hall Page was born and raised in New Jersey. She received her BA from Wellesley College, majoring in English, and went on to a master's in secondary education from Tufts, and a doctorate in administration, public planning, and social policy from Harvard. College brought her to Massachusetts and she continues to reside there.

Before her career as a full-time writer, Ms. Page taught at the high school level for many years. She developed a program for adolescents with special emotional needs that dealt with issues of truancy, substance abuse, and family relationships. This interest in individuals and human behavior later informed her writing.

It was during her husband's sabbatical year in France that Ms. Page wrote her first mystery, *The Body in the Belfry*, 1991 Agatha Award-winner for Best First Mystery Novel; the series now comprises fifteen novels. Ms. Page was also awarded the 2001 Agatha for Best Short Story for *The Would-Be Widower* in the Malice Domestic X collection (Avon Books). She was an Edgar nominee for her juvenile mystery, *Christie & Company Down East*. In 2003, *The Body in the Bonfire* was an Agatha nominee and Page's short story, "The Two Marys," was an Agatha nominee in 2004.

Descended from Norwegian-Americans on her mother's side and New Englanders on her father's, Ms. Page grew up listening to all sorts of stories. She remains an unabashed eavesdropper and will even watch your slides or home movies to hear your narration. Her books are the product of all the strands of her life and she plans to keep weaving.

"When I was a child," Katherine Hall Page begins, "I wrote little stories for my younger sister, along with poems for special occasions in the family. I've always felt the need to write."

She thinks about it for a moment. "Our house was filled with books, and the founder of *Publishers Weekly* was a member of our church . . . there was such a strong climate surrounding me that was conducive to writing. When I was in school, I had some fantastic teachers who were very encouraging abut writing. One of them wrote, 'She'll be on the best-seller list someday,' and I laughed about it. I just wanted to be a teacher."

Both were to happen in her life, eventually. "I'm really happy when I'm writing," she says. "It's hard work, but it brings me comfort, it brings me deep satisfaction."

What does the writing process involve for her? "Listen: All writers have a voice in their heads," Page explains. "I hear the voice, too, and I write what it's telling me to. Sometimes when I read back what I've written, I wonder where it came from! Writing is like a well—a lot of other people have used that analogy—you go to it, you lower your bucket, and you come up with words. I think that Madeleine L'Engle says it well: 'You just put one little word after another.' That's the process. Just listen to the voice."

Would she write even if she had never been published? "Of course! It's very personally enriching. I keep extensive journals, especially when I'm traveling or living abroad, and I'm a letter writer—a real one. On paper. So writing is always a part of me: It's not just about the books."

She's not sure what form other writing would take. "Probably something more personal," she acknowledges. "A fictionalized memoir, perhaps, or some short stories. Poetry, maybe, but I'd really only write poetry for myself." She pauses. "Besides, I'm comfortable with narrative, with telling a story. It might not be in the form of a mystery—I do that for pay!—but certainly in a way that I could develop relationships, for example."

That interest in developing relationships extends through her writing to her readers. "It never occurred to me that a character and place could become as real to others as they are to me," she confesses. "I'm always surprised by it. People will write and will ask, 'Is Faith ever going to have another baby?' for example. It's wonderful, it's marvelous to hear from people. I get at least two messages every day from readers, and it was totally unexpected."

Her conclusion? If you like an author's work, write and tell him or her! "Authors love to get reactions. Writing is such a solitary pursuit. I tell people that if they want to write they have to love being alone and indoors most of the time. Readers' comments and reactions provide a very necessary balance to that way of life."

"We are all born writers," Page affirms. "Everybody is a writer. Start with a journal, and see what happens! We all have real gifts and different ways of expressing ourselves; you just have to find yours."

SEVEN

It Takes One to Know One

There's nothing to writing. All you do is
sit down at a typewriter and open a vein.
—WALTER WELLESLEY "RED" SMITH

Disclaimer:
The characters in this book ("book" being used in the generic
sense) are fictitious. If any character herein resembles someone you
know, alive or dead, a member of your nuclear or extended family,
someone in your local or global community, your friendly librarian
or stern police chief (or stern librarian and friendly police chief), for
example, or someone you might have passed on the street heading
home from a party where you had too much to drink, it is strictly
by accident. If you are of the opinion that someone in the book
resembles you, it is likely you are egocentric or paranoid.

It is impossible to ignore the fact that characters throughout literature, in every book you read and song you hear and play you see,
remind you of people you know. Sometimes the resemblance is fleet-
ing, while other times it is downright uncanny in its accuracy. Why?

It's my opinion that there are only a dozen or so people "types" on this planet, and so it makes perfect sense for everyone to resemble lots of other people. Pick a scattered dozen celebrities and everyone you know looks more or less like one of them, at least in the eyes of a friend: Half the population, as we all know, resembles Elvis Presley.

Select a dozen personality types and everyone you know acts like at least one of them. In fact, many people think there are only two personality types, Type A and Type B. I wonder if you could pick a dozen writers and find that every other writer writes like one of them. (No, you can't *pick* the one you write like.)

It scares me how humans are so limited in true variation, and whereas in alikeness you would expect comfort and camaraderie, instead there's an insistence on identifying irrelevant differences, highlighting them, measuring them, rating them, and using them to justify one's own existence and diminish the existence of others.

I find that at the end of the day it is not when people are *in character* that they are interesting; it's when they act *out of character* and take us by surprise that they capture our attention. When a character's actions are out of sync with our expectations, we take notice, and learn that we don't know people as well as we think we do. That in turn opens our eyes to new possibilities.

Society doesn't particularly like surprises, pressuring individuals to be predictable, to follow in the footsteps of those who came before; to step out in slight, benign ways, with little risk to the individual or society. Dressing like a witch on Halloween is perfectly acceptable while practicing Wicca the rest of the year is often denigrated.

But in the fantasy worlds we call literature (or cinema, or drama, or television, or comics, or in online communities such as Zaadz), our characters go where few dare to follow: out of their comfort zone. In imaginary worlds we exalt those who walk to a different drummer—without internalizing it, without feeling a need to go there ourselves.

Years ago I wrote a poem called "The Irrelephant," the first in a series of poems I titled *Almost Animals*. In each poem, I take a familiar animal out of its element, its comfort zone, by having it question what its life is about, and making it want *more*.

In the act of asking, "Why are there so many forks in the road?", "The Irrelephant" steps out of its comfort zone, leaving the reader no choice but to pay attention. And once you have the reader's attention, you have the opportunity to get your point across.

"The Irrelephant" rocked my world. Since completing the poem, I think of it often, rereading it as I think about characters I am developing in stories, poems, even songs, and using it to move my characters beyond the obvious, to capture the attention of the reader to get my point across. The Irrelephant, in many reincarnations, appears in everything I write, sometimes as a major character, sometimes only as a bit player, but none of my writings are complete without him. The Irrelephant appears many times in this book. Think of the *Where's Waldo?* game and see if you can find him.

"The Irrelephant" was the first in a series of poems I wrote as I continued to turn to the animal kingdom to develop new, interesting, compelling, princely, or grotesque characters.

The initial point was to avoid falling into the trap of inadvertently creating characters from people I know, or read about, or see on television or in the movies. Of course, once I completed poems on a dozen assorted "almost animals," I saw everyone I knew in one or another of them anyway—in the way they looked or acted.

The innocence of these creatures created a blank slate for me. There were no preconceptions I had to deal with, no one had ever told me not to mess with the animal world, and I simply let my mind go wherever it wanted in creating my new cast of characters.

Over time I have developed a small library of these characters, and I gave it a name: *Almost Animals (but mostly human)*. The library has grown to the point where it could be a book of its own, for want of an illustrator.

The Irrelephant

The Irrelephant shook his
    head slowly
From side to side
And sighed

Not another fork in the road
He cried

I've taken the left
I've taken the right
And even walked the straight
    and narrow

I've taken the high road
And the low
The fast and the slow

And retraced my steps
To where I'd already been
When there was simply
No place left to go

And still my destination
Eludes me

And with that
He sat
On the roadside
And cried

A stereotypical
Wise old owl
Sitting in the tree

Unmoving
And unmoved
Blinked—twice

And the reflection
In the Irrelephant's tears
Caught his eye

Who are you?
The Irrelephant snorted
In his frustration
To mock my state of mind

When you have been
Sitting in that same tree
On that same branch
In exactly that same spot
For thousands of years
With a singular lack
Of curiosity

Now the Owl
Was perturbed
His night disturbed
And responded

In a most atypical
Owl rant

And in those thousands of
    years
He said
I've seen tens of thousands
Just like you

Looking ahead to where you'll
    be
And behind to where you've
    been
But never aware
Of where you are

I don't have to go anywhere
To find out who I am
And neither do you
He bellowed

The road you are on
Is as good as any
It's who you are, not where
That triggers your destiny

The Irrelephant
Looked to where the Owl sat
Once again asleep on the
    branch
And saw the forest for the first
    time

He listened for more
Unwelcome words of wisdom
But heard the forest
Come to life around him instead

And suddenly drawn by the
    need
To be part of it all
The Irrelephant rose
And at first lumbered, then
Clamored his way through the
    forest
Leaving the road far behind

Led only by what
His ears heard and his eyes saw
The Irrelephant
Was irrelevant no more!

I found exploring the idea of one's very relevance intriguing. Where relevance is an internally generated sense of self and value—and vital to mental well-being—it is confirmed externally through the approval (or at a minimum, acceptance) of others.

For any individual to truly accept their relevance, their value to society, takes great strength, a strength that for me is validated in the writing process. Writing confirms my ability to reach into my core and find that there is really something important there. For babies and young children it is enough to just exist, but as children grow and participate in social situations, their existence no longer is satisfying unless it is based on something of substance.

One thing I learned over and over again, and loved most about the dozen years that I was an elementary school teacher, is that working with children makes it very easy for me to stay in touch with my inner child and to let him come out and play. At moments like that, the desire to be relevant, and be *aware* of being relevant, simply disappears—and, with it, many of the pressures of being an adult.

Almost Animals is a collection of poems about common animals existing in various social situations. They come out and play whenever they want. They act out of character without becoming outcasts. They are whatever my pen wants them to be. It is so much fun to create a character—and look at that character as an adult, as a child, as human, and as an animal . . . all at the same time. When I am lucky I end up with a character that is part Dr. Zhivago, part Dr. Ruth, and part Dr. Seuss.

The Kangeroot

The Kangeroot
Remained steadfast
In the face of evidence
To the contrary

While his friends
Bounced joyfully

From position
To position

Never remaining in one place
For any longer than it took
To get . . .
. . . comfortable

They criticized
His inflexibility
Questioned
His very sanity

And at night
Left him to stand alone
On the position
He had rightfully claimed
for himself

To try to figure out why
He couldn't move on

It wasn't true conviction
The Kangeroot decided

For he hadn't bothered
To study the evidence

It wasn't to be different
For in the difference
He felt
The greatest pain

So it must be fear
He realized
Not fear of the unknown
But fear of not knowing

And in that instant
He took a step forward.

After I wrote "The Kangeroot," I immediately started to write its sister *Almost Animals* poem, "The Hyperpottomus." When finished, I would pair the characters in an updated, totally modern, version of *The Tortoise and the Hare*. It made me think about giving *Almost Animals* "almost relationships."

Previously, I had created my *Almost Animals* characters in isolation, to push my thinking outside the box in developing interesting characters for my stories. Since character development is the heart and soul of writing, it is risky and rewarding to move characters away from their comfort zones, rewarding because it captures the attention of your audience, gets the reader to sit up and take notice, but risky because if you push your readers out of *their* comfort zones, it's hard to predict how they will react.

Some "true and pure" artists don't care all that much about their readers, and put little energy into trying to capture the reader's imagination, attention, or adoration, because they find it somehow compromising, feel they are selling themselves out. They write what they need to write and if it actually gets read—well, that's an added bonus. I do worry, however, that such an approach may be harmful to the environment, as you destroy a lot of trees—unnecessarily. Maybe they could write books using invisible ink.

On the other hand, if you write a book, story, essay, poem, or song, or create a character, plot, or setting, and never put it down on paper, did you actually write it? What if you remember writing something, but can't remember exactly what it is you wrote? And finally, does any of it matter?

I have yet to create the race of a lifetime between the Kangeroot and the Hyperpottomus, either in my mind or on paper, and haven't decided who would win or why, or what the prize would be. In fact I'm not even sure we are talking about a footrace between these two ideologues, and if the course (mental or physical) I set up for them takes them past the Irrelephant, it's likely neither of them would finish the race at all.

Personally, I have an affinity for the Hyperpottomus, whereas I feel the pain of the Kangeroot. The Hyperpottomus is a friend more than a character or a poem, and when I can get his attention I am actively training him for the upcoming race. He is the most playful of my *Almost Animal* characters, light on his feet, quick of mind, and not weighed down by the facts of life. No, he doesn't stop to smell the roses, but he also doesn't think to ask himself if he should.

And he doesn't pay a lot of attention.

The Hyperpottomus

The Hyperpottomus sped past the
   rest of the herd
As if they were standing still:
But wait a minute, he thought
They are standing still

In the shallow pond
At the foot of hill
With just their eyes and nostrils
Floating lightly above the water line

He sped by
Feeling the thunder of his hooves
   ignite his body
Feeling the wind ripple across his
   skin
As he left the tree line and climbed
   to the top of the hill

Just in time to see the sun rise
And set the surrounding forest on fire
He watched as it reflected off the
   morning dew
And laughed out loud

Still, after too few minutes
He took off again at full speed
This time into the depths of the forest
To see and hear more of the
   morning come to life

The light filtering through the
   trees
Was now setting the forest floor
   in motion
As millions of other creatures
   woke all around him
In time to welcome the morning
   together

But then he was gone again
Out of the forest in a flash
Across open land
To the base of the hill

Where he threw himself into
   the pond
Creating a wave of such
   magnitude
That the herd, caught unaware,
   muttered and sputtered its way
Through eye-blinking and nose-
   clearing exertions

To the point of rage
(One would think)
But rage requires energy
And they settled back down
   within seconds
Just as the Hyperpottomus
   feared they would.

I struggle to create bad guys as story lines dictate. It's not that I can't make my characters do bad things; that's easy. But creating characters where negative actions are a reasonable response to who they are, and how they got there—that's far more difficult for me. Why is it there always needs to be reasons for someone to "go" bad? Did we all start out good and need something traumatic to happen to turn us to the dark side? Do all religions believe that? No, of course not. More importantly, as a writer, why is it that I look for heavy-duty reasons to create evil characters, but don't need to justify the good ones? I guess that, in my mind, *good* must be the human default.

The cAnt

The cAnt	The cAnt
Didn't	Did
And no one could make him	And no one was paying attention
So there!	So he cried
The cAnt	The cAnt
Didn't	Did again
And no one could make him	And this time
So they stopped trying	Everyone else cried.

The cAnt is my only *Almost Animal (but mostly human)* terrorist. Frustrated by poor communication skills, the inability to fit in with peers, join the inner circle of humanity, or succeed within a set of rules he doesn't understand, he finally breaks out in a big way that tells the story no one wanted to hear. In no way are his final actions a surprise to anyone (at least not in retrospect), yet they are stunningly unexpected by everyone.

To me that is the perfect character, one who lets you see everything that is coming far in advance, one who draws a detailed map, sends numerous clues and warnings to future actions, their impending behavior, and yet it still shocks you totally when he or she does exactly what they told you they were going to do in the first place. When the cAnt did, he did it in a big way.

Using animals to create characters has been a great way for me to experiment with behaviors that go beyond expected human behavior, because no one takes animals very seriously (unless it happens to be a great white shark off the coast of Long Island)—not cute cuddly dogs and cats and teddy bears, and not mean ferocious lions and tigers and bears, and not even the almost animals in George Orwell's *Animal Farm*—who might have been far more than (mostly human).

Almost Animals also lets me see where I might go if I push my own boundaries, stray outside societies presct limits, or wander down the path to the unknown.

Or have I already?

The Writing Experience

Part 7: Almost Animals

My editor has suggested an addition to my *Almost Animals* collection: the Octoplus. It certainly sounds like a good addition to me, and since I love collaboration I suggested she take it on herself to develop the character. It would be great if the "almost animals" in my barnyard had more than one originator, delivering their messages from multiple perspectives.

There is nothing more rewarding than collaborating on a project and seeing it come to fruition. So I am challenging you now, each of you, to write your own *Almost Animals* poems and see how the process helps you in developing more unique and interesting characters of your own.

EIGHT

Open Your Heart with Writing

Language is the blood of the soul into which thoughts run
and out of which they grow.

—OLIVER WENDELL HOLMES

As I mentioned earlier, during my second year of college I took, as my first-ever elective, a terrific literature course focused on the Romantic poets. The course was great because, on top of the relating well to the subject matter, the professor was totally engaged with the poets, more so than with the students, which was perfectly fine with me.

He took me with him on his trip as he read aloud and talked through the poetry of the times, bringing an entire era to life, holding my attention from the first day of class. I saw these poets through the eyes of their times, and I saw the times through the eyes of the poets. I know I should say the course changed my life, and while of course it didn't, it added to it immeasurably that semester and the next when I took a follow-up course with the same professor.

In addition, it has influenced the way I've thought about writing ever since.

If anyone wants to understand how writing opens one's heart to the wonders of the universe, from beauty, to love, to miracles, spend time with the Romantic poets who defined in almost every word they wrote what it means to have an open heart.

The first day of class I arrived a few minutes early—I even arrived ahead of the professor—not my usual way of doing things. Reverting to my more accustomed style, I sat as far to the back of the room as possible, looking around to see if I knew anyone there, or see anyone I might want to get to know. At one point, I glanced at the blackboard in front of the room where I saw the following words scribbled:

"The Spontaneous Overflow of Powerful Emotion
Recollected in Peaceful Tranquility"
—WILLIAM WORDSWORTH

Hmm. Midway through the first day of class, when I began to think the scribbling on the blackboard was left over from a previous class (I didn't even know Wordsworth was a Romantic poet at the time), I learned that the words on the board represented, for William Wordsworth, the definition of poetry.

I liked the sound of the words and the meaning they conveyed; I even liked the rhythm of the sentence, and it has stuck with me through the years. I understand Wordsworth's words, and they make sense to me; in fact, they even made sense at the time, within the very limited context available to me before we read and analyzed the poetry of the romantic period.

Today, my business blog (which I write about in some detail later on in the book) is called "Spontaneous Tranquility," a shortened form of Wordsworth's quote, because I believe those words define the way I write. Over the years they have come to represent far more than the definition of poetry: They represent the definition of writing and possibly of all of art.

Powerful emotion strikes directly to the heart, with a rush that quickly spreads throughout the body. When it is strong enough, or when you let it be strong enough, or when it catches you off guard, it takes your breath away, sometimes making you weak in the knees. When this happens to me, I have to close my eyes to try and refocus, which in turn often causes dizziness (so I open them again), and so on, but it always strikes me in the heart first.

Passing through my heart, every part of my body reacts, all at once, except for my brain, which tries to close it out. Maybe it is too much hard work for the brain to figure out what all these emotional things are that get my body to react so strongly. But after a short while it passes through to my brain, and once there, hides for a while, sitting undisturbed until my mind is ready to make sense of it and bring it back to my attention, to my recollection. The brain is the less reactive part of the body, and while your heart pounds, and your hands get damp, and your eyes cloud over, and your muscles tense, your brain mulls—the first step that eventually allows you to recollect the moment in peaceful tranquility—and translate that peaceful tranquility to the written word.

This is pretty serious-sounding stuff, so, needing some balance, let's go back to thinking and talking about the Romantic poets for a moment and see how "the Spontaneous Overflow of Powerful Emotion, Recollected in Peaceful Tranquility translates to some of the most beautiful poetry ever written.

Do you remember the image I created in an earlier chapter of the young poet struck by love passing by? Let's revisit him now.

Sitting alone out on his terrace one beautifully bright and starlit evening, a nice glass of wine by his side (not his first), and a pipe on the table next to him, Mr. Romantic Poet sees a beautiful girl walk by on her way to or from work. He has never seen her before, nor will he ever see her again. Just before she turns at the end of the street and disappears out of sight forever, she glances back over her shoulder, smiling and tossing her hair ever so slightly, and he is sure she makes eye contact for a split second—or so it seems—and he is hit with a thunderbolt directly to the heart.

For days he cannot eat, unable to think of anything besides this girl, his true love. He sits on his terrace every morning and evening, hoping beyond hope for another glance (though not for actual human contact or conversation, which would spoil the whole thing). He pines away into the night for his lost love.

Finally, some weeks later, he heads to the writing table in the morning instead of the terrace, and in this act he is freed.

She Walks in Beauty

She walks in beauty, like the night
Of cloudless climes and starry skies;
And all that's best of dark and bright
Meet in her aspect and her eyes:
Thus mellow'd to that tender light
Which heaven to gaudy day denies.
One shade the more, one ray the less,
Had half impair'd the nameless grace
Which waves in every raven tress,
Or softly lightens o'er her face;
Where thoughts serenely sweet express
How pure, how dear their dwelling place.

And on that cheek, and o'er that brow,
So soft, so calm, yet eloquent,
The smiles that win, the tints that glow,
But tell of days in goodness spent,
A mind at peace with all below,
A heart whose love is innocent!

I have no idea why, or when, or what motivated George Gordon Byron—Lord Byron—to write "She Walks in Beauty." I have no idea who he was actually talking about; it doesn't matter, I can feel the power of raw emotion in every word, and the sense of recollected tranquility that envelopes the overall feel of the poem and brings it to life.

During the summer of 2006 I visited the Uffizi Museum in Florence, Italy, and went back in time to view artwork thousands of years old, and spend time with their creators. After viewing exhibits on the main floors of the museum, I found myself wandering down to the basement where there was a recently launched exhibit of Leonardo da Vinci's work, called "The Mind of Leonardo." It was amazing. Everyone knows Leonardo loved to draw, and in addition was a great scientist, inventor, painter, writer, sculptor, and all-around Renaissance man.

The exhibition brought Leonardo to life, sharing with visitors his art and his notebooks. The museum staff had built full-size working models based on drawings Leonardo had made of the human body and the anatomy of other animals. He shared his ideas about flight and his understanding of how muscles work to enable locomotion. Leonardo was driven to understand how all things worked and his work went a step further than imitating life, he actually explained life in his art.

Leonardo's notebooks were overflowing with scribbling and drawings and notations that were incredibly complex, and if you stared at the pages long enough, trying to read his notations in the margins written at all different angles, and interspersed with diagrams and models, you could sense his brain working overtime as he looked beyond the obvious and under the surface to understand, and put into words and symbols, exactly what he was thinking. One of the things that really struck me was his use of a never-ending stream of numbers and symbols scribbled everywhere: The man had developed a language—or shorthand—of his own.

I stood in front of his drawings depicting the human circulatory system and read his notes, trying to follow the flow of the diagrams on the page; first one showing the blood flowing through the body, then another filled with strange notations and characters. As the information on the page filled my head, I had one of those special moments of understanding, one brought on by the mingling of my own curiosity and fantasy with the scientific mental meanderings of Leonardo.

As I continued to stare at the page, the symbols Leonardo scribbled throughout the bloodstream as it flowed through the body became the letters of the alphabet—and not just the letters of the English alphabet, but the letters of every alphabet in the world, all mixed together randomly. The universal language of humanity, living in the bloodstream of every human being, perfectly reasonable to come from the man often identified as the "Universal Genius."

The diagrams came to life before my eyes and I watched the blood flow from the heart to the brain where, like magic, the letters reformed and lined themselves up, first into individual words, then into sentences complete with all the proper grammatical identifiers, and finally into paragraphs and stories, poems, essays, songs, novels, plays, musicals (properly notated), and every other conceivable form of written communication.

For stored in the brain was every moment that had struck the heart with powerful impact, all hidden in the notations Leonardo had included in his diagram, and as each moment was sorted out, understood, and accepted for the wonder it brought to the individual, signals were sent out to create order out of chaos, language out of random symbols, and art out of emotion.

The artist as writer, it seemed to me then (and still does today), is the universal human being, defined by words alone, words born of pure emotion that strike one's heart with the power of a thunderbolt, emotion passed to the brain for interpretation, translation, and transformation, and finally art as it travels back to the heart for editing, to ask, "did I get it right, is there anything that needs to change, does it feel the same now as the moment you first experienced it?" and finally to pass one final test of honesty with the powerful emotion that started the entire process in motion.

The scribbling of the writer is no different than the notes of the musician or the colors of a painter's palette, or the feng shui artist's positioning of furniture. All is a part of the universal "flow" so clearly depicted in Leonardo's drawings.

Imagine all the letters of all the world's languages, and every emotion, and every human sense, and the core elements that makes us human, all flowing through the blood of every individual, with no regard for a person's race, religion, place of birth, or gender! In stark contrast to all of the unfortunate noticeable differences on the outside, Leonardo understood that each of us has the same oil in our engine, the same capacity for humanity and humility, and the same limitations.

Powerful emotion springs from unlimited and undefined resources, striking the heart first, always the heart, with impunity, often when least expected, possibly in the form of Byron's beautiful girl walking beneath his terrace, or Leonardo's spontaneous understanding of the hidden workings of the human body, or the possibility of a flying machine, or Ringo Starr's yellow submarine, or Martin Luther King's dream, or seeing the first person on the moon, or experiencing firsthand the sounds of life and the silence of death . . . or, possibly, even my attempt to share how a lifetime of writing has opened my heart.

The Writing Experience

Part 8: When You Have Something to Say, Write It Down

There are two sides to every coin, and when one is overcome with the spontaneous overflow of powerful emotion, it is a good idea to let it sit quietly in a corner of your brain before you start to write about it, and let it sit quietly in a corner of your brain before you speak about it.

This is a real life lesson as well as a writing lesson. It hit home when raising my children and when running a business. In college I learned how important it was, when writing, to let words simmer for a while in order to make sense of what you are thinking, and have the best chance to feel good that your writing is expressing your thoughts in exactly the proper way. At the time I never dreamed how that lesson translated to everyday experiences.

As a writer, I understand the process, but as a young parent and first-time business owner, I was often too stubborn to let that same process make me a more effective parent and leader. So early on, when my children did something that got under my skin, I would react immediately without giving my thoughts time to simmer. And when I first started running my own business, I was the same way.

A close friend of mine suggested that when something happened to which I had a powerful reaction, I take a step back and not respond until the following day—giving myself a chance to think through what happened and cultivate my response. I knew immediately how right that felt, and understood how slowing down my reactions would be a useful tool in many areas of my life, including child rearing.

It has been a great lesson to learn. By letting my reactions simmer overnight, the issue often became a non-issue, and I never talked about it at all to anyone. In other cases where it still felt important the next day, my responses were clearer than they would have been had I reacted immediately.

Over the years I refined the process with my children and my employees. If I wanted to talk to them about something important I would let them know a day in advance, so they would have the same advantages I had, in being mentally prepared, and having time to get at least some of the emotion out of it.

The results have been spectacular. In all cases, these conversations are far more productive than spontaneous conversations. I am ready to talk with a clear head and so is the child or employee I am talking to. Most of the defensiveness that would rise to the surface upon immediate confrontation was gone.

Opening your heart through writing is far more than just "feeling more," or "letting the sun shine in"—it's also a way to become a more effective communicator about the things in life you find most important.

NINE

Writing Is a Relative Experience

> I love writing. I love the swirl and swing of words
> as they tangle with human emotions.
>
> —JAMES MICHENER

A twenty-three-year-old woman walks up to her father at a family gathering and makes him an offer he can't refuse. "How would you like to write a book together?" she asks. "We could explore our ideas and feelings, look at our past, talk about what's going on in our lives at present, and fantasize about our hopes and dreams for the future."

As he sits there, looking at Kara, overwhelmed, juxtaposing the woman in front of him with the little girl around whom so much of his life has revolved, he knows that this is a place beyond his imagination, the breaking of new ground in a father-daughter relationship.

I remember it as clearly as if it were a single second ago: holding her in my hand minutes after she was born, looking down at her with amazement and satisfaction. The second year of her life, Kara and I spent almost every minute together as I took a sabbatical from my job to become the primary caregiver. She relied on me totally with no hint of what was to come once she mastered pushing my buttons.

After high school, Kara left for college and we no longer saw each other every day. She began to build a life without her family by her side and has never looked back. As proud as I am of the way she takes on the world and handles her successes and challenges, another part of me sorely misses our time together, the fun . . . and even the times we clashed.

After college, Kara traveled and lived away from me, and I was stunned when she walked up to me at that family gathering. "Let's write a book together," she said. "After all, you've been writing all my life, and you know how much I like to write, so let's give it a try. We'll tell each other stories; it doesn't have to be anything formal, maybe stream of consciousness. I hope to travel more in the near future and since we both use email it would be a great way to stay in touch, feel closer to each other, and probably miss each other more than we already do."

It felt like hours before I responded. I knew this was a place beyond my imagination, and that it would break new ground in a father-daughter relationship. The idea of writing together took the spontaneous overflow of powerful emotion to another level, and the hours, days, months, and years of peaceful tranquility that followed as we wrote were as meaningful and emotional as anything else I have ever done. Kara and I wrote a book together, and she titled it *I Love You Bigger Than an Airport,* which is what she always said to me as a child.

I Love You Bigger Than an Airport circumvented "really" writing to each other, for obvious and less obvious reasons. But as our writing developed, wonderful content emerged. Each of us drew a picture of our world, and our generation, from unique perspectives.

At the end of the day, we did what we set out to do. The book kept us connected for almost five years while we often were at opposite sides of the planet. Just when I was missing Kara the most, something would arrive via email to put a huge smile on my face.

She told me she frequently had the same experience. And we learned about each other, at times far more than I needed to know—but those things never made it into the book.

In many ways, our relationship up to the time we started the book was one where I was the teacher and Kara the student. Almost from the first word written that changed completely, and I was surprised at how ready and willing I was to let it happen. In the act of writing the book, we became peers in at least one part of our relationship; as peers I believe we built a lifeline for a lifetime.

Before I ever started writing with Kara, my mind traced the many possible outcomes of the project. I wanted to know where the road would lead before we got there, whether there were dangers ahead to make the experience less than we envisioned. In those very early days of the book, I tried to analyze where it would lead, but when I did, the fog rolled in. I had to accept we would take it as it came to us and find our way because that is who we are. But there was no way we were going to have the answers we wanted before we started to write. Why does life always come down to trust, and to trust you have to open your heart?

My relationship with Kara has never been about silence: It is about words. We always find words for each other, words of love and kindness and warmth—but not always the right words or the words the other wants to hear. Sometimes they are words spoken in the context of a moment rather than the perspective of a lifetime. We laugh together at our words, and we cry together over words we can't take back. Were we ready to put our words on paper, words that who knows who will read or see? When we are together, we never run out of things to say, and rarely let each other finish a sentence. Now we would finish our sentences and our thoughts and our stories, and at the least we would share them with each other.

As the book developed, my approach changed as I realized I

wanted my children to see my generation, the baby boomers, through my eyes; understand what fuels it, where I see its vitality, and how I fit into the picture. I want my children to know Neil-baby and Neil-child and Neil-teenager as well as they know Neil-daddy. I am passionately curious about Kara's generation, what drives it, even if it is just beginning to develop an identity of its own.

I Love You Bigger Than an Airport is a masterpiece, playful and full of stories of love, not bedtime fairy tales, but real-life stories recollected in peaceful tranquility. Not only stories with a message, but stories with a message to each other; messages that appear to outsiders in invisible ink. *I Love You Bigger Than an Airport* goes far beyond a father/daughter relationship and may offer a small piece of a roadmap for parents of my generation and their children, as they try to understand each other and each other's generations.

Here is my first story for Kara:

You Can't Get Here From There

In 1970, I was twenty-three, the age you are as I write this. I started out as a war baby, grew into yuppie-hood and proudly blossomed as a member of the most famous generation in history, the baby boomers.

Possibly my generation was the first to be "named" from birth (and later to be followed throughout our lives by a series of defining acronyms). Many of us "baby boomers" were born within days and weeks of each other, some nine months and a few hours after the end of WWII, when our fathers returned home to the States, victorious and needing to celebrate. It was amazing how many friends I grew up with who were born on the same day, the same week or month that I was. Too many Gemini's creating an irreconcilable imbalance in the world's population.

If there was one thing you could say about my generation in 1970 it was that we were not about "stuff." We were about choices, about right and wrong, about doing good, about communes and community, about saving the environment, and about options that had nothing to do with the stock market. We were about equality and legalizing pot, about war and peace, about the cost of free love and, of course, about changing the world and making it ours. Maybe most of all we were (like all generations before us, as well as those to follow) about fixing everything our parents' generation did so poorly, like the way they abused the environment and elected all the wrong people as public servants. We knew what the really important things were, and none of them—ever—had anything to do with "stuff."

So how did we end up being the generation that inspired the now-famous bumper sticker, "He who dies with the most stuff wins?"

There is no road that leads from there to here.

Or was it our parents who won?

Our parents, of course, were first raised during the Great Depression as young impressionable children with suppressed opportunities, and later were deeply impacted by living through the pain and suffering of WWII and the sense of nationalism that enveloped the war and the country's ultimate victory. In total opposition to our upbringing, they knew what it meant to not have stuff, either firsthand or within touching distance. They experienced a hostile environment and they raised us with a focused sense of purpose—they wanted us to live in a secure world, to have more stuff than they ever dreamed of having for themselves, and to never have to worry about not having enough stuff. Having the "right stuff" was not to be defined until much later in our lives.

But in the end we rebelled against all the things our parents wanted us to have, and all the pain and suffering they wanted us to avoid, because we didn't feel their fear and anguish. And we rebelled long and hard—the cold war belonged to their generation, and so it was their responsibility to "fix" it. The same was true for the Vietnam "conflict," although this was much more difficult for us to write off, as our friends and relatives were fighting on the other side of the world. At the other extreme, we happily took ownership of free love and communal living, legalizing pot and loving rock and roll, and delaying our entry into the real world—but somewhere along the line, as we rebelled . . .

. . .we, too, started gathering stuff—and more stuff, and eventually we had the most stuff that had ever been gathered by any generation. Today, in fact, we remain collectors, amassers, amalgamators, and consumers like the world has never seen, and still we want our own children to have more.

A lesson to all parents, including us: Be careful what you wish for!

A lot of what Kara and I wrote in this book about isn't just about us, or even our feelings. Much of what we wrote is a snapshot of a moment in time, an interesting person we met, or a random thought that we felt a need to share. There is the old saying that a picture is worth a thousand words, so is it possible that a thousand words are worth a single picture?

And here is her first story for me:

Laugh at Yourself

I often assume I have few memories from when I was little, until I start to think about them, and one by one they come to the surface to entertain me. One was that my favorite day in kindergarten was grocery-shopping day. Everyone brought in empty cartons of food from home and the teachers set them up on shelves with prices on them. We got little plastic shopping carts and Monopoly money and got to peruse the fake supermarket isles for our favorite foods.

Another memory is that we had Great Danes the entire time I was growing up. The Great Dane was my father's favorite dog, but it just happened to weigh about 100 times my weight, and could knock me over with its breath. We had a huge blue one that was fenced in and I used to torment it by spraying it with the garden hose. The dog would go crazy trying to attack and drink the water at the same time. For some reason I thought it was hysterical and didn't realize that the small metal fence between us was probably not the best protection!

A third memory that really sticks in my mind was my "talks." When I was about eight, I had this amazing room with all purple furniture, and purple rug . . . and even purple flowered wallpaper. God knows how I have any taste now. Over my dresser I had a massive purple mirror and I used to sit on the top of my dresser, legs crossed yoga style, and face the mirror. Thus began my talks. I would face myself and have whole conversations to the mirror. I remember putting a rubber bracelet on my teeth once and talking for hours about how I had gotten braces and how much I hated them. I talked about friends at school and things I wanted. I don't really remember the details of my conversations and actually I did not even think of this until my parents brought it up many years later. I would leave my door open a crack and my parents would listen from the hall, surely more entertained than I can even imagine. I can't wait for my kids to do the same—and I can also have a good laugh!

Now my father is my mirror, and I am his. No matter where our lives take us, we always seem to stay in touch by sharing little stories via email to entertain and learn more about each other and ourselves.

I plan to write with my other children in the coming years. It will keep us close and in touch, and change the frame of reference for our relationship. How many times have you heard young adults complain that parents still treat them like children, and how many times have you felt that yourself?

I also hear parents say, "No matter how old he or she gets, he or she is still just my little boy/girl." These parents are selling the potential of a relationship short. A parent/child relationship can be so much more. In writing together, Kara and I explored what that "so much more" means.

I struggled with trying to be careful as I wrote. I didn't want to hurt feelings or overstep boundaries that needed to stay in place. I was thinking in a narrow parent/child frame of reference. But after a period of time, I started to understand that "be careful" thoughts were getting in my way and I let go.

I didn't need to approach this differently from other books I wrote. I have fun writing, playing with words, sentences and paragraphs, but I don't enjoy playing with feelings. So I was careful at times, editing things that made me uncomfortable, but I do the same thing when writing in a host of other situations, including articles, blogs, and this book.

Writing with my daughter, whether or not it revealed the depths of our hearts and souls, provided a vehicle for us to entertain each other, and stay close no matter how geographically far apart we were.

My son and I talk about working on a musical together, and building a website. We will. My youngest daughter works for me in my latest venture, creating opportunities for us to collaborate as well.

Parenting includes mentoring and setting limits, but the best part of family is the everyday, nothing special, shared experiences. These experiences are rich with writing opportunities. Family diaries, another variation on note taking, are a great way to record special days spent together, screaming at each other in the car on the really long ride to vacation, watching a child participate in a sporting event, or working together making a picnic or dinner party.

In every chapter I can find another great reason to take notes!

The Writing Experience

Part 9: Putting Google to Work for You!

Google knows everything there is to know about everything, more than anyone needs to know. As a resource for writers, it is the greatest tool in history.

When you can't afford a research team, Google it. To get started, take a paragraph or two you have written and Google a few nouns. Use information that returns to build out your ideas, and make the paragraph more interesting to readers. It is not cheating, as writers research content all the time and Google is a research tool.

Here is a fun example.

I.

Bobby Donuts sat in his bright yellow '61 Corvette near the entrance to the park. Remaining in the car at all times with the engine running, he saved meter money. Alert, Bobby eyed the limo idling across the street in front of the office building that housed his target. Marcom was an attorney with a large firm that occupied most of the building. The firm made its money and reputation on asbestos-related lawsuits. A full partner, Marcom's name was on the window, but that didn't keep him from being a sleaze.

As Marcom entered the limo, Bobby revved the engine as he prepared to follow. He wondered if Marcom would slip up today,

Bobby's first day on the job. As he followed the limo downtown, Bobby made no attempt to keep out of view. The Corvette was a loud color, made lots of noise, and turned heads as he drove a couple of cars behind his target. Bobby didn't have to use the Corvette; he also had a perfectly good four-year-old Honda Civic sitting in his driveway. But he chose the Corvette for two reasons. The first was that he hated jobs that required trying to nail cheating spouses, only taking them for the money. The second reason was that he didn't think cheating was a big deal for corporate bigwigs, so long as they took care of their family. More often than not, the younger wife was hiring him to find a way out of the prenup and walk away with big money.

The limo stopped in front of a fancy restaurant where a woman came out and made her way to the car. Bobby scrambled to get his camera in position and get a couple of shots off before she got in the car. He followed the car to a nearby motel, shot plenty of pictures of the two of them going in together, waited fifty minutes, and got more pictures of them coming out together, and followed loudly as the limo went back to the restaurant to drop her off, and finally it was back to work for Marcom. Hopefully the afternoon adventure was worth it, thought Bobby.

II.

Bobby Donuts sat in his bright yellow '61 Corvette near the entrance to the park. *Corvette introduced a winging new shape in '61 and Bobby loved it. It was the first Corvette with individually adjustable seats and the seat tracks themselves moved farther back for more driving space. In addition a nineteen-percent narrower driveshaft tunnel made for more leg room, fitting Bobby's six-three frame comfortably. For muscle, the car held America's most famous high-performance engine, the Corvette V8. Quick and sharp as a whiplash, this engine had 315 horsepower with fuel injection. Just sitting in the cockpit gave Bobby an undeniable sense of self-confidence.*

He remained in the car at all times, saving meter money. Alert. Bobby eyed the limo idling across the street in front of the office building that housed his target. Marcom was an attorney with a large firm that occupied most of the building. The firm made its money and reputation on asbestos-related lawsuits. A full partner, Marcom's name was on the window, but that didn't keep him from being a sleaze.

Bobby chuckled as he remembered reading an article recently that might cut into their little empire.

President Bush yesterday called for limiting asbestos lawsuits, saying the number of frivolous cases has clogged the courts, bankrupted companies, and denied compensation to legitimate victims who've been sickened by the cancer-causing fiber.

"The system is not fair," Bush said at a forum outside Detroit. "It's not fair to those who are getting sued, and it's not fair for those who justly deserve compensation. These asbestos suits have bankrupted a lot of companies, and that affects the workers here in Michigan and around the country . . .

Marcom emerged and got into the limo. He wondered if Marcom would slip up today, Bobby's first day on the job. As he followed the limo downtown, Bobby made no attempt to keep out of view. The Corvette was a loud color, made lots of noise, and turned heads as he drove a couple of cars behind his target. Bobby didn't have to choose the Corvette: He had a perfectly good four-year-old Honda Civic sitting in his driveway. But he chose the Corvette anyway, for two reasons. The first was that he hated jobs that required trying to nail cheating spouses, and he only took them to keep rent money coming in between the fun jobs. The second reason was that he didn't think cheating was a big deal for corporate bigwigs, so long as they took care of their family. More often than not, it was the much younger wife hiring him to find a way out of their prenup and walk away with big money.

Bobby followed the limo to a familiar downtown restaurant,

Brasserie Les Halles. It was the logo that made the restaurant memorable to Bobby, who had eaten there only once, a client paying the tab. *When the logo is two cows French-kissing, you know you gotta have beef,* he thought.

The limo stopped in front of a fancy restaurant where a woman came out and made her way to the car. Bobby scrambled to get his camera in position and get a couple of shots off before she got in the car. He followed the car to a nearby motel, shot plenty of pictures of the two of them going in together, waited fifty minutes, and got more pictures of them coming out together, and followed loudly as the limo went back to the restaurant to drop her off, and finally it was back to work for Marcom. Hopefully the afternoon adventure was worth it, thought Bobby.

 ## Some Thoughts on Writing from . . . Elaine Gottlieb

Elaine Gottlieb has been a freelance writer for more than twenty years. Her feature articles and essays have appeared in major print and online publications, including the *Boston Globe, Chicago Tribune, Dallas Morning News, Cleveland Plain Dealer,* veritude.com, healthgate.com, salary.com and body1.com. She welcomes questions and comments from readers at elainego@verizon.net.

How did you start writing? Were you a child? What was the first piece that you wrote? What made you write it?

As a child, my creative expression was drawing, not writing, although you could say the two were intermingled since I made up stories about the people I drew.

I enjoyed writing poetry for assignments in elementary school. In high school, when my economics teacher gave me an A+++ on a book review of John Galbraith's *Affluent Society* and praised my writing, I thought of becoming a movie reviewer.

My creative writing started the summer after my freshmen year in college, while staying in a cozy little room at an inn in Martha's Vineyard. I loved Sylvia Plath's *The Bell Jar* and identified with it so intensely that I read it twice. There was an early poem of Plath's, "Mad Girl's Love Song" included in a biographical note at the end of the book. I read the poem endlessly and suddenly started writing my own (awful) poems.

Do you see writing as a spiritual act? If so, how?

Writing is absolutely a spiritual act; the inspiration always comes unbidden from a source that some call the muse, others might say is God. Ideas for my creative writing, which is currently essays and stories, come to me as a sentence or phrase in my mind that I feel compelled to write down and see where it leads.

The actual practice of writing—and especially editing and rewriting—is a more "rational" process. But any activity, including writing, becomes a spiritual one when you let go of the conscious mind and are mindfully present with it.

What is it that writing does for you in terms of fulfillment— making yourself whole, filling a void, connecting to something beyond yourself?

When I write, I feel uniquely fulfilled and peaceful and that I am doing what I need to do with my life. When I neglect my writing, I become depressed. Writing allows my deepest feelings and insights to surface. It clarifies the meaning of my life experiences in a way that nothing else does.

This book is about opening your heart with—or through— writing. Have you found that to be true in your own life? How has writing been meaningful to you on your life journey?

My identity is inextricably linked to being a writer; I experience life through my connection with language. Whenever I do something I love, it connects me with my heart. It is a profound joy to participate in a form of expression that has resonated so deeply my entire life. Reading was one of my earliest pleasures and remains so to this day.

Does writing make you feel more (or less) connected to others? How . . . and, if so, with whom is the connection important?

Writing is a way to share your inner self and experiences with others. It is deeply gratifying when people read my writing and appreciate some aspect of it—my use of language, perceptions, experiences, or emotions.

Do you write because you like to do it? Or is there something else that drives you to write?

Writing is hard work but when it flows it is a great pleasure. I write because it is a necessity and I feel a void when I don't. Words come into my mind that I must write down or the creative spark is lost.

Give one example if you can of how writing has opened your heart to something that has remained important to you.

I can't recall writing opening my heart to something new, but rather illuminating what I've already experienced. I treasure the new insights and deeper appreciation of life that I've discovered through writing. Describing an important experience in evocative language elevates that experience to a higher level.

Do you have advice for others exploring writing as a means of opening their hearts?

When you feel inspired to write or if an idea comes into your mind, do it. Don't let it pass. If your instincts or intuition guide you to write, do it even if your conscious mind objects or comes up with reasons why you shouldn't write or have better things to do. Write because you must and don't think about possible outcomes or gains. The best writing comes as a pure act of creation, divorced from practical concerns and ego gratification or aggrandizement.

TEN

Teach What You Learn

Writing became such a process of discovery
that I couldn't wait to get to work in the morning:
I wanted to know what I was going to say.
—SHARON O'BRIEN

In the 1970s, I was a writer posing as an elementary-school teacher, teaching fourth and fifth grade, at times in a structured classroom, and at other times in an open classroom.

Teaching is a great profession for aspiring writers because the teaching schedule gives you time to write, and because being in a learning environment is inspirational to the writing process. After I stopped teaching in 1981 I took courses at a local college and at my local high school, and I found that also inspired the writing process. My mind was getting exercise and it carried over to my writing.

Our educational system comprises a structure in which a few people succeed spectacularly, others fail to the same extreme, and most simply find a way to wander through and survive—unnoticed, unharmed, and uninspired. In public education I found this to be true for teachers, administrators, and children. It would not surprise me to find the same is true in most professions, so it would be great for people to have a business GPS to lead them out of the doldrums, to the land of success and fulfillment.

It is the majority of the children in elementary school, the group that goes unnoticed to whom we do the greatest disservice. The other children, those who fail or succeed spectacularly, or act out, are the ones that have resources thrown at them from all sides, including local, state, and federal resources.

Children in the middle, those who don't stand out educationally or behaviorally, have access to few resources. They don't *need* resources, so they don't get them, and they don't need attention, so they don't get that either. Their personal GPS won't be provided by the system, it needs to be provided by their parents or caregivers.

One of the books in this series is titled *Open Your Heart with Geocaching*. My understanding of geocaching is that it consists of wandering around the world with a sense of purpose, looking for hidden treasures via clues and coordinates provided by people who hide them.

So let's imagine that you have a personal geocaching device leading you to hidden treasures such as inspiration and knowledge. Some of these treasures are available at home or at school, but others you need to find on your own. Just type in the coordinates, search for a while (there is no reason it should be easy), and *voilà*, you find what you are looking for!

The teacher in me wanted to provide children with tools they could use to succeed, and the writer needed to develop it more and create a roadmap for caregivers to help them provide these tools to their children. The writer was the bigger thinker, but this was a project for teacher and writer to work on together.

As a proactive parent or caregiver, the first step you take is to get your child out of that under-resourced middle group and into the success arena, where they get a piece of the resource pie reserved for the best and the brightest and those who know how to manipulate the system.

I was in the right place at the right time. I started teaching in the late sixties, when there were two things going on in our country that uniquely reshaped the education system.

The first was a shortage of qualified, certified teachers in the country, which encouraged people trained in areas outside of education (many with no training in education) to take teaching jobs and fill the gaps. Once you completed a year of teaching, at least in New York State, you were granted a permanent teaching certificate in lieu of having to go back to school.

The second influencer was the Vietnam War. In the late 1960s and early seventies, teachers were exempt from the draft, and for many graduating college students philosophically against the war, teaching was a way to avoid the draft without breaking the law or leaving the country.

These two factors accounted for a new breed of teacher entering the profession, changing the face of education. For one thing, there were more men teaching elementary school than ever before, more men providing role models for children in the earliest grades, and more men influencing the direction of elementary education.

In addition, for the most part, these were educated, inquisitive, motivated young men, completely untrained in education. They were scientists and mathematicians, businessmen and artists; some of them were writers. They wanted to exceed expectations. They felt the burden of responsibility that comes with teaching, and were willing to question how things were done to find new ways to reach and teach children.

It was an exciting time to teach, a time when the system was significantly influenced by the baby-boomer generation. Some changes instituted during that time showed great promise, and others created challenges for educators.

The group of teachers I worked with was young, bright, and strong. We spent plenty of time in the classroom, and got deeply involved in other areas of public education, including administration, curriculum development, and strategic planning.

Somewhere along the line, a number of us noticed how the children of teachers outperformed other children in school. (To be clear, these weren't children of teachers in our school system, but children in our school system whose parents were teachers elsewhere and unknown to us personally.)

These children weren't typically the brightest in the school, but they knew how to turn on the system and put a positive spotlight on themselves. Since many of us were starting our own families at the time, this struck a clear chord that went beyond the classroom: We were already thinking about ways to be sure our own children would succeed in school.

After teaching ten years, and seeing this phenomena multiple times, I joined forces with Gail (also a teacher and writer, also married and with children ready to start school) to try and "bottle" what made those students stand out. We took notes on teachers' children, whose success was obvious, identified traits that made these children successful, and soon expanded our study to other top-performing children.

We wanted to write a book giving parents access to strategies we identified as being key to the success in school, and provide exercises they could institute at home to proactively move their children into the success group.

Gail and I spent years researching these children, interviewing them, their teachers and parents, monitoring their success over time. We tested strategies we developed to see if they could help other children succeed, with our own children and with parents who gave us a hand as we wrote. We named the book *Ed-Vantages*, and we gave it free to hundreds of parents to use with their children, getting positive feedback from parents who felt it helped their children move through public education successfully.

Here are some excerpts from *Ed-Vantages:*

Teachers call them "super kids." They are the children who light up the classroom because they love to learn and participate in the process. They see school, with its many classrooms and extracurricular activities, as an adventure, not an exercise to be endured or a prelude to "real life."

Super kids are not necessarily the brightest, the most artistic, or the most athletic. Instead they stand out because they are the most engaged, self-confident, and productive. Teachers want these children in their class because their very presence enhances the learning experience for the entire group. Parents want their children to be super kids because this is the best indicator that they will be lifelong learners, assets to their community, and creative fulfilled adults.

Most interestingly, we found out that there are common characteristics that flow through these children, and through their families; traits that are tangible, teachable, and universally accessible.

One of the first things we learned about these families is that they, in one form or another, create a series of "words (ideas) to live by." Some of them actually write them down and put them up on a tackboard or the fridge, while others use them in everyday speech, over and over.

It is interesting to note that when you listen to or talk to successful athletes at the professional level, their speech is frequently littered with success sayings and clichés—often seemingly trite to outsiders——but that work for them as they continue to achieve at the highest level.

So to get started we sprinkled the book with many positive quotes and sayings that parents could post on their own bulletin boards to get started. We called them "signposts." Here are a couple of examples:

Learn to live, and live to learn
Ignorance like a fire doth burn,
Little tasks make large return

—BAYARD TAYLOR

-or-

You cannot teach a person anything:
You can only help him find it within himself.

—GALILEO

-or-

Destiny is not a matter of chance, it's a matter of choice;
It is not a thing to be waited for, it is a thing to be achieved

—WILLIAM JENNINGS BRYAN

Creating this book, we merged the joy of learning with the joy of teaching; all initiated by the powerful emotion brought on by seeing children succeed, especially when you are a part of it. The joy they experience envelops everyone around them in a cloud of learning pleasure. The signposts were motivators and reinforcers for parent and child alike, words to live by that became ingrained in their everyday lives.

We created a survey for parents to assess where their family stood as an "ed-vantaged" family. People love assessment questionnaires and seeing how they compare to others.

But the purpose of this questionnaire was to change behavior by making people think about their family environment, not about whether they are doing things right or wrong, but whether they are doing these things at all. "Mental magnets" is what I call them.

Mental magnets are thoughts that the mind is told to pay attention to, and which unconsciously or subconsciously change behavior.

Have you had a conversation with someone who tells you they are having issues with a child and wonder aloud if they give their child enough attention? The first thing you did after that conversation was to go home and give your children extra attention! The mental magnet was set and you responded.

Here are questions we included in the assessment profile to show how we set magnets to help parents bolster their children's success:

Area I—Home Behavior/Attitude

- You ask your child to explain their behavior before you judge it
- Members of your family tutor each other
- You show that you enjoy being around your child while she is doing schoolwork
- You watch educational TV with your child

Area II—School Behavior/Attitude

- You communicate with your child's teacher regularly via notes or telephone
- You and your child frequently discuss what went on in school
- You seek your child's teacher's input when setting educational goals
- Your child participates in extra-curricular activities and/or school sports program

A discussion of each question on the survey reinforces the importance of each behavior to strengthening the power of the magnet, providing a rationale for the importance of each to the edvantages process.

The rest of the book provides specific techniques parents take to create ed-vantages for their family. The exercises are simple and don't take an exorbitant amount of time.

One example is for a parent and child to each keep a timesheet for one week. Both the parent and child drag around a piece of paper for a week and write down in a single sentence what they do most hours of the day. The important thing is to sit down at the end of the week and compare results. Each will be surprised seeing how the other spends their time, and will change their behavior toward the other from the knowledge gained. This exercise, done once every six months, creates many positive changes in behavior as each thinks ahead to the next time they will do it.

A writer is a writer is a writer. A writer never has to look for things to write about, but needs to pay attention to the world around him to let the words flow. The mind knows what is important, grabs hold of it, and doesn't let go. *Ed-Vantages* was written thirty years ago, and I still have copies of it, and it is relevant today. When the time is right I will give copies to my children to the ed-vantage of their children.

Ed-vantages, firmly embedded in my brain, helped my wife and I raise three children, especially after I stopped teaching to become an entrepreneur, and after we moved from the town where I taught, eliminating the "advantages" of knowing the teachers. Each of my children read *Ed-vantages* in high school and frequently teased us that we were using the "scientific method" to raise them. They would point out which chapter of the book our strategies came from, and loved seeing signposts on our fridge that came from the book.

Ed-Vantages is as much about success in life as about success in school. The silly exercises we used with our children, and the survey I have read through hundreds of times, setting permanent mental magnets, have all impacted my life, my writing, and my management style as I run companies.

The Writing Experience

Part 10: Photo Ops

One day, while teaching my fifth-grade class, individual children were giving oral reports to the rest of the class. This had been going on enthusiastically for most of the morning, proving that a great thing about teaching in a self-contained classroom is that if you are really "into" something, you don't have to stop because the bell rings sending the class to another room. When we were *into* learning we would keep going until it wore itself out and make up whatever subject we had skipped later in the day or the next day.

One of the children had conducted an experiment for his oral report. The child held a very large picture up in front of the class for about thirty seconds (which felt like a long time); then he removed the picture from view.

Next, the class was asked to describe specific things they saw in the picture, for example a tree or a bicycle, and as they called things out he wrote the list on the board. When the class had exhausted their ideas he again showed the group the picture.

Everyone was surprised both by how many things in the picture they had missed, and by how many things they had identified as being in the picture that *weren't there*.

When we finished, I asked the class to write descriptive paragraphs about the scene in the picture. They could describe the picture itself or get more into the plot, what they thought was happening, and create short stories of their own, based on the picture.

The lesson was so popular that we started doing it once a week in creative writing, with a different person bringing in a picture each week. A couple of times, we used real-life pictures—going outside and staring at a scene, for example describing everything they saw on top of a nearby hill, or describing the house across the street. It was always interesting, and no matter how hard we tried, and how much better we got over time through practice, we always missed a lot.

As a writer you are not always in a position to write notes when something of interest passes your way. So you take mental notes, and when you get to your desk you write them down from memory.

When you have done this exercise many times, your memory improves, and your notes will provide valuable content as you add new scenes or ideas to whatever you are writing.

ELEVEN

What Moves at the Speed of Thought?

Conversation is the slowest form
of human communication.

—AUTHOR UNKNOWN

"Business on the Internet," according to Bill Gates in a speech given over ten years ago, "moves at the speed of thought."

At that time, in the 1990s, many reporters and writers covering the business beat (aside from trying to figure out what the Internet was all about) were paying attention to just how difficult it seemed to be for corporate CEOs to change the way their companies worked—specifically, to improve the speed at which they embraced and integrated change to take advantage of the latest technologies.

Today, business on the Internet is moving even faster than the speed of thought, at what I like to call the speed of "pre-thought." Pre-thought can be perceived as ideation, thinking about something unconsciously before you actually start thinking about it on a conscious level. It consists of those thoughts with which your mind comes up seemingly all on its own, without you having to put any mental energy into it, ideas just appearing out of nowhere, similar to what we call intuitions, or possibly gut reactions, stream of consciousness, or even dreams. A recent book, *Blink: The Power of Thinking Without Thinking*, by Malcolm Gladwell, talks about ways in which what I am calling pre-thought can actually be used to improve performance in a business environment.

Sometimes I wake up in the middle of the night with a pre-thought and write it on a pad I keep on my nightstand, unedited, until back to sleep I go, knowing I wouldn't have slept unless I got it out of my head, but happy to wait until morning to look at it again. About half the time morning comes and I can't read what I wrote down, but once in a while a jewel of a pre-thought is legibly scribbled on that pad, and I start thinking about it consciously and building on the idea.

In business meetings and brainstorming sessions, pre-thoughts fly around the room like lightning, coming out of participants mouths before the speaker has a chance to evaluate what is being said. In a controlled environment, where everyone understands the "rules" of engagement, pre-thoughts lead to breakthrough ideas, ideas that take a company to another level, but only after they are turned into considered, thoughtful, courses of action (recollected in peaceful tranquility).

When it comes pre-thinking on the Internet, it is important to understand that the speed at which pre-thoughts travel online, and travel far beyond those who understand the rules of engagement, creates danger. Pre-thinkers don't necessarily assume the same level of responsibility for their pre-thoughts as they do for considered thoughts.

In controlled environments, where participants are clear about the goals of the meeting, and understand random ideas are being tossed around to stimulate discussion, brainstorming is a powerful business tool, but in the frontier of the Internet, where there are no *understandings* of how words should be taken, we find all of a sudden that we're held responsible for "thinking out loud," our musings, our stream of consciousness, responsible in ways that show how misunderstood our words can be.

For that reason, we have an editor who reviews everything our business posts on the Internet, from web pages to web blogs to e-newsletters and online marketing materials. It is not because we want to control what people in the company want to say, but rather to be sure people are saying what they want to say, posting thoughts they feel empowered to take responsibility for. Once we post words on the Internet, we need to assume full responsibility. Once posted, other people reading them will assume that our words reflect time spent pondering the message, and that our conclusion(s) are drawn from, at minimum, a reasonable level of evidence and / or research.

Therein lies the best and the worst of the Internet as it relates to writing. For many people, writing on the Internet is the spontaneous overflow of powerful emotion and to hell with recollecting in peaceful tranquility, and for them the Internet moves at the speed of thoughtlessness. These people frequently experience the pain of taking such a position. Politicians, business leaders, educators, and others have all been dutifully punished by pre-thoughts published on the Internet that have returned to haunt them.

You would think that business leaders would be savvy enough to avoid the pitfalls of having embarrassing content posted on the Internet. In fact, the opposite is true. There is an Internet company (whose name cannot be printed in a family book) that generates a high volume of site traffic and significant advertising revenue, by posting corporate memos being leaked by disgruntled employees. These embarrassing messages were never "meant" to reach outside the company. But at the end of the day, retribution is painful, and very expensive—read lawsuits—for transgressors, not only for the individual, but also for his or her company. Many memos posted for all to read on this site negatively affected the stock price of companies and the careers of the careless employees who wrote them, including CEOs.

For writers who use the power of the Internet to distribute content, those who post not in haste, but in the same measured way they publish letters to an editor for their local newspaper, or important business memos, for the majority who take responsibility for their words, the Internet is a powerful vehicle for research and collaboration and, in the end, for highly considered, and often brilliant content distribution to thousands upon thousands of people at a speed that comes close to being instantaneous.

I've been writing on the Internet for ten years, ever since I started running Internet-based companies, and I assure you writing on the Internet is a different kind of animal from any other medium, and not only because you have to be careful in what you say.

For me, as for most people, email started it all. It gave me a way to communicate faster than ever before with people all over the world, although today the speed pales in comparison to messaging in real time on cell phones. Email is still a medium on which I rely, especially for the way it builds and stores content and conversation over time, maintaining the original thread of a conversation. A friend recently mentioned to me that he has found when he emails me, he gets a response back from me faster than when he leaves a message on my voicemail.

In addition to email, today I write website content, blogs, and online marketing content, both for myself and for clients. I blog as a way to share business thoughts with my customers and other leaders in my industry—read me, if you're interested, at neil. blogs.ewaydirect.com.

I also collaborate online with my editor as I write books and business documents, but I do this in protected areas not available to the public. When it comes to actually posting content I have written on the Internet, I do it in the following way: I never write directly in public spaces online, and I rarely post anything on the Internet the same day that I write it, unless it has been reviewed by my editor. Whatever I have written, I reread it the next day; hopefully when I am in a state of peaceful tranquility, and if I still feel that it merits being posted I go ahead and put it online.

You can't write for the Internet the way you write off-line, because people don't read the way they read off-line. They don't read novels online in bed before turning out the light for the evening, they don't read Internet catalogs in the bathroom (yet), and they don't read newspapers online on their long train commute to work, at least not in the same way they read newspapers off-line (many people check the news headlines on their handheld devices from the train on their way into work).

More importantly, people don't read in a linear direction online, one word after another, one page after another. They use links to fly from one piece of content to the next adding an exciting new dimension to the entire reading process, and a unique set of challenges for Internet writers.

Some confusion arises from the totally misunderstood, yet frequently used Internet term "browse"—confusion between what you think intuitively that it means and the reality of the behavior it produces. On one hand, people love to talk about how they browse the Internet. "I was browsing the Internet last night while sipping a nice glass of wine," or "I was browsing at work when I had nothing better to do." Employers, of course, complain about employees who spend all their time browsing the Internet when they *do* have so many better things to do.

Browsing the Internet sounds like a pleasant, leisurely activity, when it is anything but. Most people don't browse the Internet at all, at least none that I have seen—they pinball the Internet. That sounds different, doesn't it? Browsing sounds like what I do when I go fishing. I sit in the boat, drop a line in the water, enjoy the sun and the smell of the sea, wait a while to see if I get any bites, and start to nod off. Catching fish isn't essential to the nature of the experience. Or to me browsing sounds like something I do on the golf course. I hit the ball in the woods and browse around looking for it, until I give up and drop another ball, only to hit that one in the woods also. Browsing my way through a round of golf (or walk in the woods as I call it) takes me five hours. I also browse store windows when I tag along on shopping trips with my wife and/or children.

I never browse the Internet.

Technology exists today that allows researchers to sit in front of a computer and "watch" people, in real time as they browse the Internet, move from page to page, site to site, search engine to search engine, using links to move them seamlessly wherever they want to go. Using this software can help you understand how to write effective Internet content. Here is what you would see:

For the most part, people spend fewer than ten seconds on any given Internet page before moving on by clicking a link. This is hardly enough time to browse much more than a few pictures, a couple of headlines, and maybe a sentence or two of text. Just as happens when reading a newspaper, unless something on the page jumps right out at them, their eyes travel from the upper right hand corner of the page straight downward, rarely looking to the left side of the page where most sites place their navigation links. Either something grabs their attention quickly, or they are gone.

When they arrive at a page containing content that actually holds their interest, they rarely stay there a long time, averaging maybe thirty seconds, before they take additional action, either clicking on another link, signing up for something, printing information, or filling out a request form. No one I know, watching site visitor after site visitor move around the Internet in this manner, would rightly call this behavior "browsing."

"Pinball-ing" is a far better description.

One marketing writer, Seth Godin, decided to sell his books online as free downloads. All people had to do was go to his website and either read the book there, or print off hundreds of pages and read it off-line at their leisure. In part, he just wanted to see what people would do, but also he did not really believe posting the book on the web was going to attract people who actually would want to read the book online. Seth did believe people would print the book, or parts of the book, directly off the Internet to read, and he was correct.

But that was only the start. Many people who printed Godin's book, after printing all or part of his book online and reading it, would still buy the book, either because they wanted a copy that would last for future reference and browsing, or for gifts. In addition, lots of people sent their friends to his site to see the book, and some would print the book, and others read parts of it online, and surprise, surprise, many would buy the book.

Godin said sales of the books he offered free on the Internet were actually higher than sales of similar books he hadn't offered online for free. On top of people reading and printing and buying, his strategy built plenty of buzz and spread the word for him, sending people flocking to his website or to the nearest bookstore to pick up their own copy.

Writing for the Internet is different than any other writing you do. Once you accept the fact that you have to be careful, the opportunities are enormous, and make writing a lot of fun.

Just think, for example, about how link streams create a new paradigm for writing. Sure, they add complexity, but based on what we talked about earlier in terms of how people read on the Internet, it is a fundamental skill to success. When writing web pages, you need to consider the fact that this is a totally new and different way to develop your message or story line. If you ignore links, they take people away from your content and you lose them. But if you use links to guide people through multiple content pieces you have written, it will help them get where they want to go quickly. Links not only take people from page to page, but also help them jump around within a single content piece, skipping over areas that are of no interest.

When you build a website, or write content for a website, always consider all of your link stream options. It's similar to playing chess on a 3-D chessboard rather than a flat board. Your strategy and moves using links create many alternative directions for your content that need to be considered in order to optimize their value to the reader.

Build links into all of the content on your site because they create the shortcuts (think speed) people want and expect. The links enable the pinball effect of Internet browsing and create advantages to site owners by keeping people on their sites longer, keeping them moving from page to page within a site, always creating easy ways for people to find the content they are looking for, and finally make purchases or request information. On a well-written website, people move from page to page quickly, taking advantage of well-designed strategic shortcuts every step of the way to get where they want to be more quickly. But every step of the way, with every link they use to jump from page to page, they should be following a well-developed story line of your creation.

People don't read Internet content from the top of the page to the bottom, they actually read from link to link, so as a writer you have to plan your story line in multiple directions, not only from paragraph to paragraph, but also from link to link, and you need to understand how to control, or at least take into consideration, all of the navigation choices the reader might make.

Link logic is a new science every Internet writer needs to understand. Once you have written content that contains links, it is vital to follow the link path of all the links you have included, to be sure they get people where you want them to go, and to be equally sure you haven't sent them away from the rest of the content you have written, never to return, without having a good reason to do so. Drawing a good navigation map that plots out all of the links and their respective paths can help you visually see where your site visitors are going to be going.

And when you are writing for the Internet, don't put the good stuff off to the end, like they always do on television, because if you do that on the Internet, most of your audience will never get there.

The World Wide Web is so enormous that it creates a multitude of writing options, with content for websites only one of many ways the Internet is the writer's dream.

There are other forms of writing the Internet enables that are conversational in nature, and collaborative, including writing as part of interest-based communities such as user networks and/or blogging. Even though these are frequently spontaneous forums, writers still need to consider their words carefully and understand that once words are posted on the Internet, there's no taking them back, and no way to control how many websites might post them to their audiences.

The beauty of special-interest online communities and blogs is that they create a powerful way for people to share interests and ideas, and often influence public opinion, that in turn influences business decisions and even political policy on a local or even national level.

When you first decide to participate in the forums, remember to write at your own speed and don't get caught up in the speed of the Internet, although this is often easier said than done. You could write a blog, or respond to a community content thread, and receive responses to your post within seconds. When that happens, instead of feeling pressured to respond immediately to someone you are sure is just sitting at their computer holding their breath waiting for you next post, take your time, consider your response, and post it when you are sure you are good and ready.

Keep in mind that you are writing your way through multiple layers of communication at one time. While you are building your own content thread and your own argument, at the same time your words are part of a group conversation and a group argument. The group thought can and will shape and mold your own communication on the fly as you write, and if you get caught up in the flow you might end up somewhere you least expected to be or wanted to be. So when you are blogging or taking part in an interest-based community, take as much time as you need to develop your ideas, since you are usually talking to a small group of people who are very engaged in what you have to say.

Currently I am running a business engaged in providing Internet-based software to companies to help them market their products and services successfully via email. There are a lot of challenges involved in e-marketing, including the most obvious two, spam and mail filtering. My corporate blog frequently addresses these issues, and is read by marketers as well as by business leaders in related businesses. As the blog develops, or as I in turn read the blogs of people reading mine, I get to see different perspectives on issues all of us are dealing with, and become smarter about my business. Blogs are typically short and to the point, updated frequently, and are open-ended as to where they will eventually end up.

Here is one example of my blog:

What is the biggest challenge facing Internet marketers today?

Over the course of the last month I have read at least twenty times (and spoken to numerous people in the online marketing arena) about how the biggest challenge facing Internet marketers today is deliverability. Smells fishy to me, like a red herring sitting in the sun too long. But I must admit that the power of marketing comes through loud and clear when companies in the deliverability business, seeking your dollars, have managed to convince the world that deliverability is the issue . . . when it isn't.

The biggest challenge facing online marketers has been, is, and will continue to be customer acquisition. It is frustration with the pace of acquisition and the scalability of acquisition programs that has caused marketers to take poorly conceived acquisition shortcuts, alienating consumers, and at the end of the day making it more difficult to get their messages delivered to in-boxes.

Customers with well-thought-out and executed acquisition programs (and there are many examples) might build their lists slowly, surely slower than they would like, but their mail gets through to in-boxes without paying bounties and delivering incredible return on investment.

Don't be thrown off by the marketing gurus asking you to spend all your money on improving deliverability: Spend it on improving your acquisition programs and your lead to customer transition-marketing programs . . . and deliverability will become a nonissue.

Even though you likely have a captive audience when you write a blog, and you certainly have all the time you want to build your argument, it's important to keep it short and to the point. People arriving to read your blog have likely been pinball-ing around the Internet, checking out the half-dozen blogs or so they look at each morning for new postings, and you don't want to put them through too big a shock at one time. They do a quick read, hopefully respond at some point with a thought or two of their own, and come back frequently for updates (or subscribe to an RSS feed and have it delivered). A blog is a living, ever-changing document.

If you find a blog or two that you really like, sign up for them so you can be alerted every time new content is posted to that blog, as soon as it is posted. Just click on the button that says "RSS Feed" and you'll find directions there. This is an example of still another part of writing for the Internet that differentiates it from off-line writing, the idea of "push" and "pull" technology. Pull technology involves writing content to pull—entice—people to visit your or web page or blog, to see or read or even hear what you have to say . . . and possibly to respond.

For writers, there is lots of good news when it comes to opportunities on the Internet, even though it is the "other" news that most frequently *makes* the news. The other news arises from the fact that whatever you put out there on the Internet—your words, ideas, pictures, etc.—is there forever. There is no such thing as "no backsies." It sounds like a pretty simple concept—for people to be careful what they post online, but obviously it isn't.

Think of the people you know or have heard of or read about in the newspapers whose careers or personal lives have been seriously damaged by things they, or others, posted on the Internet. The Internet moves faster than possibly even Bill Gates imagined, at the speed of pre-thought, a speed that encourages thoughtlessness.

All of my life I have successfully used writing as a way to reconcile my thoughts, and in so doing, have frequently torn up what I wrote before anyone ever got a chance to see it. I would write down what I wanted to say to someone in a fit of anger or frustration . . . and the act itself of writing magically, therapeutically, relieved the frustration, so the words never had to be spoken or delivered. In business I would write plans and strategies, and then think out loud, in the end often coming to the conclusion that I was way off-base. I always had the luxury of filing it in the circular file and starting over another day. And then there were those elementary school preadolescent love notes that thankfully no one ever saw . . . My spontaneous outpourings, had they been shared with others without having had the time for peaceful recollection, would frequently have led to embarrassing moments—or worse. I'm glad I had the opportunity to avoid taking them live. I'm glad I didn't deliver them or rush them into print, or post them on the Internet.

Gates may have underestimated the speed of the Internet some ten years ago, but to me the speed of thought is certainly fast enough.

So if the real value of writing on the Internet isn't about the speed, and if it isn't about just having another medium a writer can use, what is it?

Here's what my answer is: The Internet brings people closer together than any other form of communication. I'm not talking about people I already know, people I could pick up a phone and call, but people all over the world, people with interests similar to mine—such as other writers who want to share their ideas and their writing experiences, both one-to-one and in communities, forums, and critique groups. These are people who understand why I write, who understand that I often have no choice but to write, and who understand what it feels like when the words just aren't there.

And there's a lot to talk about. The world of writing just doesn't always make sense.

When I'm in the middle of writing one thing, other ideas are trying to attract my attention, other books, other characters, other plots. When I'm between projects, though, it seems they have faded into the fog and I can't find them, no matter how hard I look. I find that particularly frustrating, but I have learned (through talking with other writers I've met online) that it is in fact quite common. Go figure.

When you post content on the Internet, it acts like millions of tiny magnets, attracting people who are interested in what you have to say, people from all over the world, twenty-four hours a day, seven days a week.

Bottom line? The Internet brings people together, and that feels good.

The Writing Experience

Part 11: A Lesson in Business Writing

Business writing doesn't have to be intimidating. Just read through the list below and follow the instructions provided at the bottom of the page.

Conflict handling, integrative decision-making process, feasibility alternatives, win-win strategy concentration, behavior influencers, coercive power, monopolistic competition, production, surveillance, quality control, requirement cycle, one-man show syndrome, crisis environment, microenvironment, interface effort, project life cycle, observance protocol, adaptive negotiations, solicitation cycle, fixed-price incentive, phase up/phase down, reallocated disposables, scope objective, preconceptual advisement, implementation executables, change management, executive initiative, career diversification phase, client/consultant relationship, technical/business interface, personal success barriers, intuitive objectification, dalliance management, preventative communications, ideological absence, attitude adaptation, managerial integration, stress impact, job insecurity, paperwork, concrete work, homework, work schedule, work-around, managerial microcosm, time killers, time-management cornerstones, organizational matrix, multimanager conflict, harassment dispersement, interdependency implementation, flexible commitment, resource criticality, constructive channel conflict, destructive compliance, quadrant architecture, constructive orientation, leadership modeling, indigenous misunderstanding, managerial indulgence, recrimination abstinence, people skills.

Just add verbs, adverbs, prepositions, and modifiers to taste.

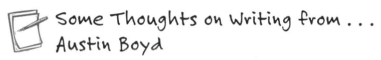 Some Thoughts on Writing from . . . Austin Boyd

A Navy pilot, nuclear weapons officer, and spacecraft engineer, Austin Boyd flew three thousand hours in war and peacetime operations, designed satellites, and built classified systems to track terrorists. A world traveler, NASA astronaut finalist, and inventor with multiple patents, he served in key Navy space assignments before retiring to Huntsville, Alabama, where he lives with Cindy, his wife of twenty-eight years, and their four children. In addition to writing the Mars Hill Classified series (including *The Evidence, The Proof,* and *The Return*), Boyd has also penned dozens of technical articles about space issues and has written award-winning poetry. He can be reached through his website, austinboyd.com.

Do you see writing as a spiritual act? If so, how?

When I first started writing, no . . . it was not spiritual. I had a deep spiritual hunger inside me, a hunger never satiated because my parents did not raise us in a church setting. We attended briefly in my early teen years, and then stopped as abruptly as we began. Not until I came to know Jesus as a personal savior and friend did I see writing in a more spiritual light, but even then, just as a kind of gift.

Today, I am convinced that I have a spiritual gift that God intends to use in a mighty way. Writing is spiritual for me, as though the Holy Spirit gives me ideas, provides insights, provokes new concepts, and helps me pluck plots and characters from the tapestry of the day around me.

I wondered for forty years, "Why? Why do I feel this incredible drive to put words on paper?" I felt like I could understand the insane pressures that drove the hero of the movie *Close Encounters of the Third Kind* to plow up his yard and build a mud mountain on his dinner table, trying to express the incredible images that flooded his mind. I have the same problem. I've written and written for the years since that first poem, shifting from poetry to technical writing to articles, then on to fiction. I can't stop the words, like an artesian well rising out of the depths, overflowing every day.

So yes, I see writing in a strongly spiritual light. This is where God prepared me to be, molding me carefully for forty years. I understand a little of what Moses felt after wandering in the wilderness for so long, to find the Promised Land. That's what I did, plot and wander and prepare for forty years to be ready for this mission. Fiction author.

What is it that writing does for you in terms of fulfillment— making you whole, filling a void, connecting to something beyond yourself?

I'm a cabinetmaker as well as an author. I build reproduction period furniture from the colonial and early American periods. I love to take a raw board and pull a piece of art out of that wood, presenting it to my wife or others and creating joy. Writing has the same fulfillment for me.

I pull ideas into some form while I'm driving or exercising, then I turn to paper in order to plot out the possible threads and get excited about the possibilities. But when I finally start writing, I write to get it out, to express that story, like pulling the furniture out of the board. I said that the passion to write is like an artesian well, always flowing, and if dammed, will overflow its banks. It can't be stopped. I write to get the ideas and stories free, and to see what they look like when I pull them out of a yellow legal tablet or piece of white paper.

This book is about opening your heart through writing. Have you found that to be true in your own life? How has writing been meaningful to you on your life journey?

Poetry and fiction both give me that sense of personal expression. Technical writing was also fulfilling, to see completed prose published in a journal or magazine, but I didn't express anything personal in that technical writing. I love fiction and poetry because I do get to open my heart. My poetry, in particular, was used to reveal inner emotion on a regular basis, whether I was writing about the one girl I cared about in high school and college, or struggling with the growing-up problems that surrounded me. I poured my heart out in poetry.

Fiction is different. I pour my heart out there too, but I can hide the motives better. Each character gets to say things that can never be attributed back to my feelings by anyone but me. I know what those characters are thinking, why they did or said what they did. But readers will probably never make the connection. I get to express opinions and pour out feelings in a way that is therapeutic. I suspect others write with the same motive.

Writing has been meaningful to me because, in a sense, it defines my life journey. I see now that all the passions that drove me early in life, to get selected for astronaut, to be a Navy pilot, to work in technical science areas, were all passions placed in me by God to prepare me for the day I would write in the way that I do. I thought I was on a journey to NASA and space, or to science, but in fact, God was molding me to be a writer. How wonderful it is to see that now, after so many years.

Does writing make you feel more or less connected to others? How, and if so, with whom is that connection important?

The negative side is that writing *disconnects* me from my family. Sitting at the computer takes time . . . 750 hours per novel. I write at four thirty in the morning to get more time with my family when they are awake, but there's no disputing . . . the effort of writing disconnects me from my wife and teenage children. That hurts.

Writing *connects* me, too. It connects me with those who read, and I'm thrilled, at a peripheral level, when I hear that people read my books and liked them. But the real connection is with those who really digest my work, people who look for the hidden meaning, the motivations of the characters. Readers who become so ingrained in a character that they ask me "What do they like to eat? When were they born?" That connection energizes me . . . passionate fans that are lost in the story just like I was. I have a few dozen loyal reviewing fans and an editor (Linda Nathan) who are such friends. When we are both talking about John and Amy Wells (my protagonists) like they are real people, that energizes me most.

Do you have advice for others exploring writing as a means of opening their hearts?

Yes, two bits of advice. Lots more, actually, but there's a practical limit to what you'll let me say, and what others will pay to read.

First, write for God and His glory, not for money or fame or publicity. Even after what I've been through, a deeply spiritual journey seeing that God was preparing me for forty years to craft fiction, I find that I get caught up in monthly sales figures and marketing fundamentals. Put Jesus first and all the rest shall be added unto you. He promises that.

Second, once you are writing for God, hone the skill He has endowed you with. Invest in yourself. Don't just write and throw your work across the transom. Take some of your hard-earned money and pay for an editorial review. Get a freelance editor you trust, and pay her to kick your teeth in, repeatedly. Learn the craft of writing as best you can, not just from books, but from hard experience.

If you felt God calling you to be an evangelist, you would have to proclaim the Gospel over and over, many times with no sense of success, but honing your presentation and your heart to be able to read the passion of your audience and to put God's promises in words that would touch those you meet. It's the same with writing. Don't fail to practice, and don't hesitate to put your writing out in the marketplace for critical review, to better learn this thing called writing.

I am passionate about investing in your craft, paying others for blunt criticism that you can't always get from an amateur critique group or friends. I grew best through this freelance editor process. God gave you the words, but He also gave you the responsibility to perfect your craft to better serve Him.

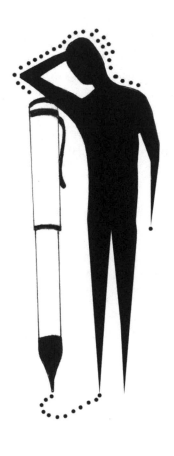

TWELVE

You Write
What You Are

Fill your paper with the breathings of your heart.

—WILLIAM WORDSWORTH

One of the things I think about when writing is whether or not it really gives me insight into the *real* Neil. As a child I was seriously into sports: Was that the real Neil? These are important questions, because I have always found that the clearer the vision I have of myself, the better I feel and the more successful I am in life. Sometimes the vision is crystal clear and other times I walk around in a fog. The interesting thing is that writing doesn't always clarify things for me in ways I would hope it would.

Sometimes writing can put me in the middle of the deepest of fogs. Many times while writing this book I felt hopelessly lost, out of words, rereading chapters and wondering where the thoughts I was reading came from, or why I had bothered putting those words on paper at all. And yes, there was a lot of balance, and times when I felt the words clarified everything and I knew exactly what I was writing, and why.

I originally titled this chapter "You Are What You Write," but it simply isn't true. You write what you are, and that is different for a number of reasons.

First is that when I don't know who I am, I can't write, words won't flow. Writing releases the fog, but only when it is good and ready. For the time being, my mental magnets are occupied elsewhere. I have to do things to free them up, usually by realizing that my attention is on a business or personal challenge that I have to deal with—and dealing with it.

Once I do that, I am ready to write again. It sounds easy, but the process of just understanding what is going on can take a long, frustrating time. To speed the process, I go back to writing notes, notes to myself, my employees, friends, and others. Note writing almost always takes me out of the fog and leads to clarity.

You write what you are, and you become more of what you are when you write, and that is how it should be.

Many authors need to separate themselves from their characters, openly defend themselves, go out of their way to point out that their main character is nothing like them at all—exactly the opposite, in fact, of who they are. They're not sure they even *like* the character very much, and if he or she were a neighbor, they wouldn't be friends. That may be true, but at the end of the day, you are what you write.

And nowhere is that more true that in a book series like the Open Your Heart series.

I do know the main character in this book, and he is not totally fictitious, at least some of the time. I am a writer. I am a family man and a businessman. I still like sports, most frequently as a spectator.

For most of my adult life, two themes have followed me from pillar to post. The first is that I move a lot, dragging my family kicking and screaming with me. I relocate, change houses, upgrade, downsize, empty one nest only to fill another, flipping houses the way most people buy shoes. Real estate is the way to the American dream.

I am not, however, a gypsy in the true sense, in that I don't ever travel far from my roots. In fact, I have lived in two cities in thirty-five years, but within those cities I have occupied twenty different houses. At times it caused my family confusion (frequently expressed in the form of tears) when schools had to be changed and friends were lacking, but mostly it was a source of friendly ridicule from family members, friends, and relatives.

When my children were young, I had a hard time explaining all of the moving from one place to another, moving to a house needing updating, finally getting it exactly the way we wanted it, only to sell it and move to another house that needed updating, and so on . . . But by the time my oldest child reached high school, they had all simply stopped asking why, maybe finally starting to understand their parents' odd addiction, but it didn't stop me from trying to explain it to them anyway. Via writing, of course.

Genetic Gypsies

Did you know that "wanderlust" (not to be confused with "wonder lust") is a genetic trait passed from family member to family member, dating all the way back to prehistoric humans? Our forebears, the enlightened cave people (at least once they had invented fire), had to move frequently and usually at a moment's notice just to stay one step ahead of both their human enemies, and the less-than-friendly very large, very mean, very hungry beasts roaming the neighborhood. Never did they stay in one cave long enough to have it become an identifiable home (yes, I know, they did draw some pictures on the walls, but you can tell just by looking at these pictures what a hurry they were in).

And in all the years since, encouraged by a broad set of wanderers from gypsies to nomads to the ever-expanding Roman Empire and more recently the California gold rush and Woodstock, humanity has been drawn by the belief in greener pastures (or just different pastures) to the point where today we need to explore the cold, harsh, unfriendly, world of space just to satisfy this genetic hankering.

I'm also not sure that you, my children, were ever informed that wanderlust is a genetic trait that may or may not skip generations, similar to multiple births. In your family, on your father's side, your grandparents moved into a house on Long Island when Dad returned from WWII and stayed in that house until they retired. Your great-grandparents on the same side, however, proudly portrayed wanderlust at its best. They moved from state to state, and from coast to coast, frequently enough that their kids would rush home from school every day just to see if there was a moving truck at the curb. Of course, in that particular situation, their wanderlust was encouraged by business failure, debt collectors, and legal maneuverings.

And so, after skipping a generation, the wanderlust trait was passed to your father with the expectation that he would carry the torch with dignity—far and wide to as many places as possible. It's hard to forget the time, oldest daughter, when you were on your way home from college for vacation and realized as you got close that you didn't know where we lived and had to call to get directions. What were we thinking, you asked, did we expect you to follow the scent from the previous house? And how about the time even I got so confused that I drove home from work one evening and into the driveway of a house we hadn't lived in for many years? But, all in all, wasn't it fun to have so many housewarming parties, go back to school every year with the ability to invite friends over to your "new" house, frequently have another room to decorate, and enjoy spending a few months exploring the house and the neighborhood?

I think about whether all those moves will make it easier for you, my children, to move about as an adult, from abode to abode, or if you will be happier to learn here about the likelihood of the trait skipping a generation, to know that you will in all probability, unless you marry someone on the other side of the skip, settle down in one place and never have to think about packing boxes, sending out new address cards, enrolling your children in a different school, forgetting where you live or missing your exit on the highway. Plus, in all likelihood, you'll always know exactly where your siblings are—since they won't be moving around much either. An additional benefit will be that you won't have your friends always complaining to you that there is no longer any room to keep you on the correct page in their address book.

The only question that will always stay in the back of your mind is—will I be able to find my mother and father?

The second theme that has remained comfortably by my side throughout my adult life has been the fact that I always seemed to be working with, or focused on, things that had to do with helping children. After college I became an elementary school teacher for a dozen years, teaching fifth and sixth grade in a public school district in New York. In my next career, I built a small chain of furniture stores selling—what else? Children's furniture.

Changing careers again ten years later, in the late 1980s I finally put it all together, melding my desire to help children and families with my addiction to relocating. I started what was to be my first of three Internet companies, a research company called the School Report, which provided relocating parents with the information they needed to help identify school districts that could best meet their children's needs.

You write what you are.

It was when I was creating the School Report that, for the first time, three important themes of my life converged: writing, relocation, and childhood education. Over the years, writing had become more and more important to me; I stopped relocating as frequently, and I became more immersed in the online business world, and somehow this all reawakened my need to write.

One piece of the service that the School Report provided to relocating parents was *A Kid's Guide to Relocation*. Nothing is harder for children to deal with than moving to a new town, or a new school, and trying to fit in and make new friends. At the School Report, we had early access to relocating families, often a year or more before they were actually going to move, and so I felt that we had the opportunity to share our experiences and help those parents make the move as comfortable as possible for their children.

The introduction to the book explains it as follows:

Emily and Mike are moving to another town. Their mother told them last week that she found a new place for them to live that would be closer to her job and give them more time together. Mike says he is excited. He is a good baseball player and knows he will find a baseball team and other kids to play with as soon as the season starts. But Emily, a few years older than Mike and in junior high school, feels very differently. She likes her friends, her teacher, and her school. She doesn't want to leave the place she has lived for most of her life.

Moving is an important life change, and as you see everyone in a family doesn't feel the same way about important life changes. Each of us looks toward a new school, neighborhood, friends, and teachers from a different point of view. Each of us has a different set of tools we use to deal with life. Most of us have mixed feelings. We are both excited and scared by the change.

The *Kid's Guide to Relocation* tried to help parents in two distinct ways. The first, as you see above, was to help parents understand what might be going through their children's head as they thought about moving. The second was to provide parents with concrete things they could do to help their children negotiate the change and have it become a positive experience for them. Teachers have a unique perspective that can help parents help their children adjust. Here is an example of one of the things the book recommended parents do to help their children:

Sizing Up Your New School—The Walk-Through

Long before you are ready to make your move, take your children for a walk through the new school they are going to be attending. Do it at a time when school is in session so they can see the other children in action. Often a school will provide an escort through the school, which is helpful because it gives the children a chance to meet some of the teachers and students in a friendly atmosphere.

Let your guide know of the particular interests of your children so he/she can improve their comfort level by letting them know they are not going to have to "give up" things they really like to do because of the move.

Don't be in a rush; plan on spending an entire afternoon in town. If you finish early at the school, go to the local mall or shopping area so your children can see familiar shops, or shops similar to the ones they have in their current community. Just giving them a feel that life is similar in the two communities is often very helpful.

Finally, before you leave the school, gather as much written information as you can about the school(s) your children will be attending. You will use this information both to get your children excited about some of the "new" opportunities offered in their new school district, and to be sure to enroll them in programs they want to take part in. Once they are enrolled, the move becomes more real to them, and they can begin to get excited about things they are going to do once they move.

A final thought is that you shouldn't do this "walk-through" once and forget about it. Your children will enjoy going a second time when possibly the fact that they had been there before will lower their anxiety and free up their minds to think better, ask more questions, and take in their surroundings in a more relaxed atmosphere.

This *Kid's Guide to Relocation*, although of modest length, was a great manual that really met a need in a fairly transient society. It was distributed to thousands of relocating families, and the feedback was always positive. We heard great things from both children and their parents—how it had made their move less stressful.

In addition, they said, it gave them a positive perspective on how to think about the move, prepared them for the challenges, and helped them find the way to look at the move as an opportunity, rather than as a necessary evil. This last piece was a common theme in the feedback we received.

The *Kid's Guide* was successful, I believe, because there was nothing that I was more prepared to write. I had been a teacher for twelve years, I had moved frequently, had three children of my own, and I had personally experienced their stress about moving many times. I had a really good understanding of how families think about relocating, and over time found ways that really did make relocating easier for the entire family. In fact, for many families, the workbook enabled them to make the move a positive adventure and a lot of fun.

When words flow from your heart, you write what you are.

The Writing Experience

Part 12: Get on Your Hobby Horse

The Open Your Heart book series is unique in that it is written by authors who share how hobbies have enriched their lives . . . and show you how they can enrich yours. Hobbies meld with work and family and recreation to create identifiable intersections in life, as well as to help you select a positive direction.

Roads: Driving America's Great Highways is Larry McMurtry's book about cruising America's best-known highways from one end to the other. McMurtry is the perfect tour guide, offering nonstop trivia about towns he passes, and people he talks to at various stops. He provides historical perspective to his travels, especially interesting information about famous (and infamous!) writers who lived or are living along his route. McMurtry took a favorite hobby, driving, and shared his experiences in a well-deserved bestseller.

Identify intersections in your life, places where work and family and hobbies meld together, to motivate your writing. These intersections point to ways in which your life makes sense, grabbing your attention, and ultimately providing the fresh perspective that is the foundation of great writing.

THIRTEEN

Memories Are Made of This

Keep a diary and one day it'll keep you.

—MAE WEST

Recently I overheard a young friend, a "seriously casual" writer, comment on how she was turning fifty and that meant it was time to start writing her memoirs. It made me wonder if there is, in fact, a time in your life when you should change your perspective and start looking over your shoulder instead of looking to the future.

Even if there is such a time, it seems curious for anyone to think about writing their memoirs when they might have traveled less than halfway through life . . . unless, of course, they know something I don't.

I am aware that our life expectancy is currently in the area of seventy-five-plus years. I also suspect there are a lot better ways to measure how long you have lived than by how many years you have been breathing.

Particularly important, far more important than a chronological timeline, is *how* you have lived your years, how much sharing and caring you have packed into each day, and how much you expect to live in your remaining years. Not every minute in a life is created equal.

The optimal situation would be to write your memoirs for this life once you have gotten to the next one (assuming you have time and nothing better to do). Since that's not possible, let's use the scientific method to determine when to optimally write your memoirs. Try this:

Having experienced childhood in my own right, and having raised three children of my own, my initial scientific assumption is that the first year of life is barely worth a month of what I'm going to call "memoirability." When you watch adults start jumping up and down in delight while exclaiming, "Did you see that? She looked at me!" or "I think she blinked!" . . . well, you get my drift. Plus, few of us can remember a single second of our first year of life, so we have to rely on hearsay from people who are totally biased. This is certainly not a time in my life I plan on including in *my* memoir.

The next four years, at minimum, are spent *learning the basics.* This includes everything from crawling to standing to falling and finally walking; to babbling, to mumbling, to talking and to screaming—over skinned knees, over pinched fingers, and over not getting what you want—to beginning to understand that words and numbers are interesting.

This stage also includes learning how to manipulate your parents into giving you exactly what you want at all hours of the day and night. So given how busy you are mastering these life skills, surely there is little room to experience anything "memoirable." All in all, my scientific analysis calculator gives those four years a memoirability value of one year.

One-third of the following twelve years are spent in school, one-third of them are spent fighting with parents, and only one-third is memoirable. I include in this calculation the likelihood that you had a teacher in high school who changed your life and was the impetus for your becoming a rocket scientist instead of a drug addict, but this balances nicely with all the questionable things you did in high school that you don't want *anyone* to know about.

Graduating from high school in the nick of time for you and your parents, you head off to college, the armed forces, or work, and your memoirability quotient now takes off. You are still painfully finding out that there is more to learn, despite your own dearly held opinion that young adults know everything. (One of my favorite bumper stickers reads "Hire a Teenager While They Still Know Everything.") But now it is back to basics one more time, finding out what you suspected all along—that twelve years of school prepared you poorly for life. Taking it all into account, your twenties shape up very nicely and take a huge jump in memoir value, and that decade contains enough important events to be worth eight years to your memoirs.

I hope you were taking notes.

The analogy continues to, no doubt, a chorus of groans. Here you are at the ripe old age of thirty, and you have accumulated a grand total of twelve years of experiences worth talking about in your memoirs, or at least thinking about including in your memoirs, experiences that your readers *might* be interested in hearing about.

The thirties are great. You are an adult, and have become the person you most disdained in your twenties, a thirty-year-old. You discover with some amazement that your life didn't end, after all; it is, in fact, just beginning to build up a head of steam. Your career and your family are taking off. A year is worth a year, a day is worth a day, a kiss is just a kiss, and a smile is still a smile, but by forty you've somehow managed to accumulate ten more memoirability years. It's a beautiful thing.

Now, when you reach forty (way before you wanted to), you

find that something wonderful happens: Life continues to get better, each day a bit more valuable. Something new has come into your life, a new way of thinking—it's called *perspective*. You sense that you are a part of something bigger, a community, maybe, and it makes you pay attention to the world around you and how you relate to it because it feels important. Perspective is worth lots of memoir points, a year is worth more than a year, and by fifty you have accumulated an additional fifteen memoirability years, upping your total to thirty-seven years and one month.

The momentum you are now experiencing will continue to accelerate exponentially, or at least accelerate with a fractional exponent, so you still have at least fifty more memoirable years to live and therefore at fifty you aren't close to being halfway there.

I probably wrote all of that to justify to myself that I am almost ten years past the ripe old age of fifty and I haven't yet begun to even *think* about beginning my memoirs . . . or have I? Even though I haven't yet thought of *writing* my memoirs, I *have* in fact taken notes for most of my life, and there's no reason I shouldn't be accumulating them, reading through them, writing notes (not memoirs) to fill in the gaps and protect against the fact that I might soon start forgetting things faster than I can learn new things. Maybe the most important thing I can do right now is just put them in a safe place!

Actually, I believe that writing notes *can* ward off memory problems, for a number of reasons. One is that writing things down on paper eliminates old mental magnets, things your mind has struggled to stay on top of, pay attention to; it therefore makes room for new ones. In addition, the act of writing is mental calisthenics, and exercise does as much to keep the mind in shape as it does the body. The mind can build up a nice sweat just thinking.

Throughout my life, I have shared my stories with family. In the book I wrote with my daughter, I tried to share what it was like growing up as part of the baby-boomer generation. My family fully understands how my reflections represent my particular experiences and unique prejudices concerning events that took place during the sixties and seventies and eighties, the late sixties being the time when I left the nest permanently. It is important to me for my children to have a sense of my generation that goes far beyond the way we are depicted in books, magazines, and on the television. It's most important for me to give them a sense of me as part of the generation they have come to know as the baby boomers, much as we needed to have a clear perspective on our own parents' generation, who shall remain nameless, but whose lives were so deeply affected and molded by the Depression and WWII.

I am willing to stand on my notes, whether or not I ever actually go through the process of putting them into a formal memoir. Maybe my children will do it for me.

In our forties, as I mentioned, we gain perspective, and in doing so we enrich our daily life. We start to see our lives as part of a community, understand more deeply how our life entwines with others around us, and how we affect the larger communities of which we are a part, both locally and globally. Perspective is a good thing.

In our fifties we notice another phenomenon entering our psyche, appropriately named selective memory. The perspective we gained in our forties starts to become a bit more subjective. (Selective memory is not to be confused with selective hearing, an affliction infuriating to wives and mothers and girlfriends that affects almost all men who are both over fifty and who play golf and watch football games!)

Selective memory is a powerful tool that enables us to rearrange our past in such a way as to raise it in stature, making it all that much more desirable. When it comes to writing memoirs, selective memory is probably important, but its value is questionable.

Since I am not yet thinking about writing my memoirs, I shall rely upon my note taking to add content to this book, and as a way to view my life. I make no guarantees that when I finally get around to writing my memoirs I won't feel differently.

Here is another example of note taking that talks more about the community I call my generation. I was trying to define when a generation begins and when it ends, thinking about how it does not include all of the years of our life, only the high memoirability years. I wrote a number of essays at the time I called "Bookends." Each of them looked at different aspects of life and tried to use that perspective to define the parameters of the baby-boomer generation. I am sure that all baby boomers would take offense at the thought that their generation is still not a major influencer of world politics, finance, and social policy.

One of the essays used two presidents to define the bookends of the generation, Kennedy and Clinton. A second defined the bookends in terms of wars, recounting the Vietnam War and Iraq. And finally I looked at the business world, talking about how advancement in technology defined the bookends of the baby-boomer generation, from Microsoft to eBay and Google. Here is the essay on the presidents.

Bookends

Two Democrats sit like bookends spanning the vital years of my baby-boomer generation, presidents Kennedy and Clinton. Both of them captured the imaginations of my peers like few who came before or after them. In addition, they embodied what our generation has come to look for in Democrats, including the character flaws that jump off the pages of the history they wrote.

Both Kennedy and Clinton were bright and articulate, their intelligence blazing across the country. They were the center of focus for their administrations, so there was little talk of how important it might be to surround themselves with the "right" cabinet members. In addition, their charm was magnetic, displayed both at home and throughout the world. They were the photo opportunities of their time, for leaders everywhere. When they were in the Oval Office, many of us believed that anything was possible.

Kennedy and Clinton also in many ways represented the political "children" of our generation as a counterpoint to the Republican "adults." They played on the job, got in trouble for their antics, and were a real part of the sex, pot, and rock-and-roll experience. They were the closest we ever came to taking the campus experience of the sixties to the White House. It is not impossible to picture either of them leading a demonstration on the steps of any major university. And in addition, they just couldn't control themselves. I mean, after all, how hard is it to behave yourself for the relatively few years you will be in office? Obviously for them it was much harder than one might think!

Of course they were also different from each other in many ways: maybe the most interesting difference is that Kennedy was deeply loved by the majority of the country while Clinton is deeply hated by a vocal minority. Kennedy had the advantage of being able to go about his day-to-day business without having to deal with the distraction of seeing his sexual exploits in the press, as they didn't really come to light until after his presidency. At the end of the day, though, if I close my eyes and think about them, as long as they kept their pants on, each of them possessed a spirit of leadership that energized the country and made us feel good about living here.

From generation to generation, each of our personal archives is highlighted by a series of bookends—important events that help define the parameters of a generation. Maybe events that will play into the bookends that define my children's generation will include George "Dubya" Bush, the Internet, and terrorism; forty years from now . . . will the back end of their generation, their other bookend, be defined by global peace, prosperity, and humanity? Is that too much to ask for? Maybe, but I have high hopes based on the incredible humanity I have seen in my children and their friends, and peripherally their generation.

So now that I have written my note on how I think about writing memoirs at the age of fifty-nine, I'm going to put the entire idea of a memoir on the back burner where it belongs. Instead, I am just going to continue adding to the notes I started writing in fourth grade. And although I am unlikely to share my notes with others (this book being a notable exception), I won't destroy them, but instead leave them behind for others to read, my children, my friends, and who knows who else?

There will be lots of long notes and short notes, cute notes, funny notes, and seductive notes. My notes, read chronologically, might just show a maturity of perspective as I reached my forties—and most certainly the immaturity of selective memory as I got older. In addition, they won't all be pleasant; you might see mildly paranoid notes and scared notes. The really bad notes, the ones that I'm not quite ready to face or put down on paper, I promise to keep in my head.

To my young, barely-approaching-fifty writer friend, I'd suggest putting off any further thought of writing or organizing your memoirs for a while longer, at least until you pass the halfway point—or are ready to approach the project with a smile on your face.

Just keep taking notes as if your life depended on it.

After completing this clinically scientific study on life expectancy, in my own case I have decided to wait until I am sixty to start any serious thought of writing my own memoirs. And the scary thought is that if you are reading this, I've probably reached that point, as I will reach sixty in the summer of 2007. Today I am either sitting at my desk organizing my memoirs or just writing notes.

Hmm . . . which one, do you think?

The Writing Experience

Part 13: The Loudest Day in America

February 9, 1964, at 8:55 p.m., four months before I would graduate from high school, and three months after President John F. Kennedy was assassinated in Texas, was undoubtedly the loudest moment in American history.

For months the tension was building throughout the country, and for the fifty-five minutes leading up to the American television debut of the Beatles on *The Ed Sullivan Show*, it had become almost unbearable.

And Ed Sullivan used every ounce of his genius to make sure he got the most out of the moment. Before each commercial break he announced who would be appearing after the coming onslaught of commercials, the first time being the jugglers, the singers, the dancers, the acrobats and the Beatles—all coming up after the commercials. Before the next set of commercials it was the jugglers, the dancers, the acrobats and the Beatles, and so on and so forth throughout the show.

There was a conservatively estimated 73 million people watching *The Ed Sullivan Show* that night, with 99.9 percent of them tuned in to see the Beatles for the first time, including every girl and woman in the country between the ages of eight and twenty-nine, as well as quite a few women older than that, but who would never admit it.

They called it Beatlemania, and once it hit the States, it never stopped. The Beatles, as it turned out, were no one-hit wonder, and they endured years of outrageous screams from their wildly enthusiastic female admirers, not to mention that they changed rock and roll forever.

I watched the show with my parents and my two sisters, as well as a couple of their friends, and therefore got to experience the full impact of the moment firsthand, watching them scream to the point of tears running down their cheeks, as they were reduced to squirming in their seats like quivering bowls of Jell-O.

The Beatles didn't have to actually sing that night, as it is likely no one could hear them over the noise, but they did, and they lived up to every bit of the anticipation, and if it is possible, they probably exceeded expectations.

Ed Sullivan built dramatically to his ending. He took every opportunity to create additional tension, to tease the audience, to make outlandish promises. Most importantly he delivered on the promises, with the greatest ending in show-business history.

Keep that in mind every time you write. Think of Ed's commercial breaks as the ends of each of your chapters. Build into each of them a bit of anticipation about what lies ahead, either in the next chapter or perhaps something to look for later in the book.

At the same time, don't lose sight of the big picture, of the promise you made to the reader on the book cover and in each previous chapter. A great way to do this is to write down what you want the three or four most dramatic moments in the book to be. At the end of each chapter, glance at these notes, and try to weave a tease about one of them into the last paragraph.

This is a great way to both remind the audience where you are taking them, and building their curiosity and *need* to learn. It is you constantly reworking the theme of telling your audience where you are going to take them, taking them, and finally letting them know where they have just been.

An additional benefit of working this way is that these notes you have taken on what you want your dramatic moments in the book to be remain in your mind as mental magnets, and over time will become enriched and deliver added value to your writing process.

FOURTEEN

When Two People Think Alike

Every writer I know has trouble writing.

—JOSEPH HELLER

"When two people think alike," my friend and business associate David is fond of saying—hopefully with his tongue in cheek—"one of them is totally unnecessary, redundant, in fact."

We typically have this conversation a couple of times a year, and almost always in the context of a business discussion. As obvious as it seems, there are many times when it is a valuable observation, and it is not a bad rule of thumb when thinking about staffing a business or when thinking about setting up committees for everything from a condo association to a fundraising event.

I specifically remember a time when the two of us were sitting together in a business meeting with a bunch of typical corporate types, and whenever one of them was speaking, the others would be sitting around the table in their matching suits and ties, doing their best imitation of bobblehead dolls. Since David and I usually expressed differing viewpoints (both from theirs and from each other's) on almost all of the items on the agenda, we left the meeting with little hope that a deal would be made any time in the near future with this company.

It's easy to nod your head. People (especially businesspeople) like to see you nod. It shows that you understand. It shows that you agree. It shows that you aren't thinking. Every time I'm tempted to nod, I think of those bobblehead dolls.

In a world where fitting in with the corporate culture is held in high regard, and conflict resolution is a term associated with "other companies," the corporate culture that David and I espoused was not particularly well aligned with that of the company with which we had just met. Neither of us, at the time, was particularly disappointed that a deal was unlikely to happen. By the time we exited the building our thoughts were on to the next challenge.

And it wasn't going to involve nodding.

A number of threads have run through this book, note taking and collaboration being two of the more important ones.

Life is basically a collaborative process and writing is no exception, where collaboration enriches, for me, both the execution and the end result. My fondness for working with others during the writing process, especially people who think about things differently than I do and add talents to projects that I don't have (illustration and musical composition, to name two), becomes especially apparent when I see multiple talents melding together to create a full-production musical, or an illustrated collection of poems and stories, or turn novels into books-on-tape or a television production.

And simply bringing a book to market, which is not something that is done simply at all, requires the efforts of multiple people (whether you like it or not), from the writer to the publisher, marketer, printer, book distributor, bookseller, and others. When a talented group of committed people works together toward a single goal, the end result is always a step above what is produced when each works independently.

In the specific case of this book, which is part of a series, the complexity is even greater; all our marketing efforts have to consider both the book and the series of which it is a part.

Collaboration is not a natural skill for the writer. The writer is often portrayed as a solitary figure, alone against the world. Writers like being unavailable, free to listen to their muse. Many writers express, in public at least, that they're drawn to writing in solitude, feeding on their aloneness, remaining out of pocket, and out of the mainstream as much as possible, and leaving the *rest* of the work to others for whom they have great need but little regard.

There is a similar stream of thought in the medical field (although no doctor would admit it in public), where you have diagnosticians and surgeons. The diagnosticians think of themselves as the brains of the outfit, and frequently regard the surgeons as plumbers. We're all in this together, and the faster we realize that, the more we'll accomplish.

The most important relationship the writer has, and the one that can add the most to the product, is that which he shares with his editor.

Let me tell you a little about my editor, Jeannette, who has worked on this project with me from the beginning. In fact, she is the one who encouraged me to write the book in the first place.

Jeannette is a brilliant writer and published author in her own right; she's another contributor to the Open Your Heart series, as well. She rarely nods. She and I do not think alike.

What does an editor do? Jeannette does a lot more for me than making sure my writing is technically correct—although I would have to say that the proper use of language is as important to her as any other piece of the process.

A couple of paragraphs ago, I talked about writers liking to write in solitude and remain "out of pocket." It's the child in me that made me keep that phrase there as written, and (I am ashamed to admit) it was simply to push Jeannette's buttons. The first time she saw the phrase, she pointed out that I was using it incorrectly, the true meaning being "having to pay for something out of one's own funds (pocket) upfront," not being "out of touch."

My contrarian point of view is that using the phrase to mean "out of touch" has become so common, at least in the business world, that it should stand as written. Since Jeannette technically works for my publisher and probably has the final say, I hope that if you actually go back a few paragraphs to look for it you'll find it still there. [Note from the publisher: Aside from the usage issues pointed out by Jeannette, it's a cliché and should also be removed for those reasons as well.]

Of course, correcting spelling and grammar is not collaboration. Pointing out the "big picture" places to me, the places where the book needs improvement, where it isn't flowing properly, or where it could use a fresh look—*that's* collaboration. Asking me to leave the big picture view and focus on certain details that need my attention is also collaboration. "Here is an area that needs to be developed further," she'll say, or "this section is awkward," or "I think you are not clearly making your point here," or the particularly cruel "do you have any idea what you are trying to say in that paragraph?" . . . it's all collaborative.

Jeannette doesn't provide concrete changes to content; that's my job. And she never tries to change my *voice,* an author's most valuable asset. But in the simple act of pointing out problem areas to me, she sets mental magnets for me to think about, and as I review the areas she points out, the book gets better.

In every case, the places she pointed out? They had problems that just jumped off the page at me . . . once I paid attention to them.

Jeannette, being a writer herself and having been through it all, also seems to be able to differentiate when solitude is the necessary prescription (well, I never said there *wasn't* a time and place for it), and when collaboration is the way to go.

Of course, when a writer is deeply involved in a project, there are lots of times when it's best to be locked in a room somewhere on an isolated island with no other humans within ten thousand miles—but with, of course, Internet access and a well-stocked refrigerator! (When Jeannette takes off to that isolated island to write, she doesn't have a well-stocked refrigerator or Internet access. She walks a mile or two with a bucket over frozen tundra to fetch water for cooking. We view pain and depravation differently as it relates to the writing process.)

Either way, though, what I'm talking about is the aloneness that it sometimes takes to let the words flow—or, sometimes, get out of the way and watch them spill over the keyboard like a coming flood.

But writing is rarely that easy and never that easy for long.

Once the flood has subsided, it may be hard to find a single word that moves you to the next sentence or the next chapter, or the next book, for quite a while. When you try to get back on track, there are many distractions that can sabotage your project—maybe characters from other books you have started writing, or plan on writing in the future, who call out to you for attention. Jeannette knew that talking through what was going on in the process made it easier to let go of these distractions and get back to the business at hand, and so we've talked about this book—a lot.

I am very pleased to say to David, as well as all those bobble-head businessmen out there, that my editor and I are successfully working our way to the finish line, on schedule, pretty much without agreeing on *anything* beyond the overriding project itself.

Politically and socially, Jeannette and I exist about as far apart as Gandhi and Attila the Hun. I am a proponent of the world getting to where it needs to go on the backs of the individual, while she believes it will take the strength of community. These two viewpoints are not *necessarily* mutually exclusive, though—I have a wonderful feeling of community myself, so long as it is a community of no more than two people. Once it is larger than that I have difficulty wrapping my mind around it.

Most important, at least to this book, is that Jeannette understands what the end result must be, look like, feel like, in order for the book to be both interesting and valuable to the reader. She has helped me get there while at the same time improving the overall quality of the writing itself. It seems that I am often, to her dismay, hardly serious enough at all about anything beyond the words themselves, so I am ready to cop out on that front and leave that to her.

This is the first time I've ever worked with an editor on a book from start to finish, and I must say that I have no idea at all how the *typical* writer-editor relationship works—or *should* work. In my case, the collaborative value Jeannette brings to the table is enormous and comes in the two major areas mentioned previously. The first is concrete: the editing of my writing for proper grammar, structure, and appropriate usage. A writer's thoughts come across better when his manuscript is clean of errors.

The second area is less concrete but of no lesser value. She points out areas I need to work on, in her relatively low-key manner, using a technique that has morphed into a simple code that works well for both of us. She recommends that I *pay attention* to some specific area of my work, nothing more.

She understands that the only way to pay attention is to *open your heart*.

I find the process has delivered value to me in the way I now approach everything I am writing, including things that are never going to be published or professionally edited—things like poems and songs and business plans. I know enough to ask others to read something I've written and point out to me areas that don't flow correctly, or where they don't fully understand what I am trying to say. Just a comment or two like that is likely to help me find areas that in fact do need additional attention, and the end result is better, clearer writing.

The concept of *voice* is also what this final chapter is all about. *Don't let your voice be redundant* is the initial advice given in the chapter. At the same time, always know and maintain your own voice, and fight to keep it—as loudly and clearly as you possibly can.

The second message, brought home by my editor, is this: Don't try to change another person's voice, or convince them to come over to your side; instead, *pay attention* to it. Let each voice speak its piece.

I have another good friend who is fond of using an expression initially passed down to him from his father, an expression that I love and feel ties the dual themes of this chapter together perfectly. It emphasizes people's ability to maintain their own voices, think about things differently from each other, maintain their individuality to avoid becoming unnecessary or redundant, and use that individuality constructively in meetings, conversations, and other creative endeavors.

My friend Steve likes to say, "You can't put your head on someone else's shoulders." It's another variation on *pay attention*, in that it is far more important to hear what a person is saying than to get distracted trying to figure out their motivation. Each person has the sole responsibility for the head that rests on her shoulders, as well as the words that come out of her mouth, a responsibility to not let her head, or words, become redundant.

David, Steve, and Jeannette, each with their idiosyncratic expressions, sum up for me what this book is all about and why all of the years I have spent writing have been such an overwhelmingly important part of my life.

In writing, I sometimes search for, and at other times find out, who I am. I look at where I have been and what it has meant to me, and peek down the road where I may be going.

In my writing, I often find what is truly important to me, what I need (as opposed to just wanting) to say, and sometimes I even learn *why* I want to say it. Whether anyone reads what I have written or not, I can often entertain myself by listening to my own voice. Even though I am a Gemini, I thankfully have no one else around who nods his or her head when I speak through my writing. Even my other Gemini self, whose head shares a common set of shoulders, doesn't agree with me very often.

But it isn't all about me, not by a long shot. My writing has shown me new ways to look at what other people write, new ways to hear their voices. I can pay attention to what they are saying without trying to put my head on their shoulders.

The more I write, the more I am learning to pay more and more attention to not only my words, and the words of others, but also to other people and the world around me. And that alone makes it all worthwhile.

The Writing Experience

Part 14: Blogging with the Authors

DreamTime Publishing is the publisher of the Open Your Heart series. Visit the website, dreamtimepublishing.com, to see the books in the series and learn a little about each of the authors. In addition, you can participate in each author's individual blog, including mine, which are posted on the site. This creates an opportunity for you to understand what makes each of us tick, and learn about the blogging process by becoming an insider.

Blogging with the authors in the series and reading their books provides you a broad perspective on how the Open Your Heart series takes its theme further than any of the individual books can on their own.

Meg Bertini, our publisher, welcomes you to the blog section of the site with the following message:

> Welcome to the DreamTime Publishing blog.
> We love books, all books, even books not
> published by DreamTime!
>
> We have two main purposes for our blog:
>
> One is to host an online book club, where
> readers can respond to our thoughts about
> books by their favorite authors.
>
> Two is to allow readers to post questions
> about relationships, job issues, etc. We
> in turn will give a bit of informal input—
> remember that if you want professional advice,
> you should seek a professional. We are not
> holding ourselves out as experts on any of the
> topics we discuss. Our advice will more times
> than not be based on books we've found to be
> especially useful, books that will hopefully
> allow you to resolve underlying, recurring
> issues.
>
> Thanks for having a look. Comment early and
> often, and happy reading!

Resources

Critique Groups

Nothing can replace a critique group for giving you a valuable perspective on your work. A local one is best, as you're actually interacting with real people, something writers sometimes need to do. Check with your local chain or independent bookseller and see if it hosts a critique group. If it doesn't, and you don't want to start one, then you can check your local paper or Craigslist and see if there are any around.

There are a few Internet critique "groups" that are worth checking out, either in place of or in addition to a local group:

- IWW: The Internet Writing Workshop (internetwritingworkshop.org) includes both a general writing discussion group and groups where you can submit and critique work in a number of different genres (novels, short stories, flash fiction, nonfiction, romance, poetry, and young adult & children's writing). In addition, there's a remarkably useful group here called Practice in which, each week, a new writing topic is assigned and later critiqued.

- Zoetrope Virtual Studio (zoetrope.com): You've probably seen either the magazine or the collections of short stories in your favorite bookstore. This is Francis Ford Coppola's workshop, and obviously scripts and screenplays are the stars here, but you can also get quite useful critiques of novels and short stories as well.

- Forward Motion for Writers (fmwriters.com): Although there are critique groups here, you'll also find an amazing number of places to discuss your writing by genre, from Christian fiction to horror and dark fantasy to poetry and experimental prose. Well worth checking out.

Books

Practical Guides: This is the section that you can probably discover by yourself, either online or at a bookshop, so I'm not going to spend a lot of time discussing any of these books. Some of these come out on a yearly basis so make sure that the version you get is the most recent. Where the author changes with each edition, we did not include the author's name. See which one(s) work for you and check them out:

- *Children's Writer's & Illustrator's Market*
- *Guide to Book Publishers, Editors & Literary Agents* (Jeff Herman)
- *Guide to Literary Agents*
- *How Plays Work: A Practical Guide to Playwriting* (David Edgar)
- *Novel & Short Story Writer's Market*
- *On Writing Horror: A Handbook by the Horror Writers Association*
- *Poetry Writers' Yearbook*

- *Selling Your Story in 60 Seconds: The Guaranteed Way to Get Your Screenplay or Novel Read* (Michael Hauge)

- *Tax Deductions A to Z for Writers, Artists, and Performers* (Anne Skalka)

- *The American Directory of Writer's Guidelines*

- *The Playwright's Survival Guide: Keeping the Drama in Your Work and Out of Your Life* (You gotta love that title!)

- *The Renegade Writer's Query Letters That Rock: The Freelance Writer's Guide to Selling More Work Faster* (Diana Burrell, Linda Formichelli)

- *The Short Screenplay: Your Short Film from Concept to Production* (Daniel A. Gurskis)

- *How I Write: Secrets of a Serial Fiction Writer* (Janet Evanovich)

- *Wordsmithery: The Writer's Craft and Practice* (Jayne Steel)

- *Writers' & Artists' Yearbook*

- *Writer's Market*

- *Writing a Great Movie: Key Tools for Successful Screenwriting* (Jeff Kitchen)

- *Writing a Screenplay* (John Costello)

- *Writing Magic: Creating Stories that Fly* (Gail Carson Levine)

- *Writing Movies: The Practical Guide to Creating Stellar Screenplays* (Gotham Writers' Workshop)

- *You're Not Fooling Anyone When You Take Your Laptop to a Coffee Shop: Scalzi on Writing* (John Scalzi)

- *Writing Spiritual Books: A Bestselling Writer's* Guide to Successful Publication *(Hal Zina Bennett)*

Less Practical, More Creative:

- *On Writing* (Stephen King): One of the best pieces of advice I've read anywhere is here: never be without a book, carry one in your pocket, read, read, read.

- *The Tao of Writing: Imagine, Create, Flow* (Ralph Wahlstrom): Wahlstrom also explores opening one's heart, taking the reader on a journey within and searching there for inspiration through imagination and creativity. Also includes writing exercises.

- *Writing Alone and With Others* (Pat Schneider): This book takes the reader along on Schneider's creative journey, encouraging every step of the way. This is more about finding your own writing comfort zone than about giving specific advice.

- *Escaping Into the Open: The Art of Writing True* (Elizabeth Berg): "What you need most," writes Berg, "is a fierce desire to put things down on paper." She talks about both fiction and nonfiction in ways that make her own words come alive—and make the reader work harder to see that the same happens for him/her.

- *Your Life as Story* (Tristine Rainer): Remember all my notes? Rainer shows you how to put them into a coherent narrative.

- *Catching the Big Fish: Meditation, Consciousness, and Creativity* (David Lynch): Director-producer Lynch (*Twin Peaks, Black Velvet*) discusses how he captures and develops ideas through meditation.

- *Writing the Fire: Yoga and the Art of Making Your Words Come Alive* (Gail Sher): A combination of practical advice and inspirational wisdom, exercises and thoughts that will stay with you long after you read the book.

- *Why I Write* (George Orwell): Three essays and a short story sum up the inspiration of one of the twentieth century's greatest writers. Be prepared for his political views, but take his wisdom no matter what you think of them.

- *Writing to Change the World* (Mary Pipher): The best-selling author of *Reviving Ophelia* tells writers that it is their duty to save the planet and its people; she offers practical outlets for changing the world, from blogs to letters to the editor, and culls quotes from the unlikeliest of sources.

- *On Writing Well* (William Zinsser): A classic tome on writing nonfiction, dealing with the usual suspects but also with science and technical writing, business writing, and sports and humor writing.

- *The Art of Fiction* (Ayn Rand): Either you like her or you don't; either you believe in what she has to say, or you don't. There's nothing in between. Rand sees fiction as deriving from a belief in free will, and therefore "romantic" in nature. She urges writers to look for "countless concretes under your abstractions."

- *Write Away: One Novelist's Approach to Fiction and the Writing Life* (Elizabeth George): The author says it best: "I have a love-hate relationship with the writing life. I wouldn't wish to have any other kind of life . . . and on the other hand, I wish it were easier. And it never is. The reward comes sentence by sentence. The reward comes in the unexpected inspiration. The reward comes from creating a character who lives and breathes and is perfectly real. But such effort it takes to attain the reward! I would never have believed it would take such effort."

- *Writing Down the Bones* (Natalie Goldberg): Goldberg affirms that the rules for good writing and good sex are the same: keep your hand moving, lose control, and don't think.

- *Bird by Bird: Some Instructions on Writing and Life* (Anne Lamott): One of the *de rigueur* texts for writers, Lamott echoes some of my own thoughts: "to have written your version is an honorable thing."

- *The Best Spiritual Writing 2000* (Philip Zaleski, ed.): The introduction to this book, written by Thomas Moore, is breathtaking. Read it for that alone.

- *Zen in the Art of Writing: Essays on Creativity* (Ray Bradbury): Not the author you'd expect to tackle the topic, but the book is thoughtful and will slow you down to look at your own creative process.

- *Zen and the Writing Life* (Peter Matthiesson): The author discusses his own development as a writer and how meditation enlarged and clarified his sense of purpose.

- *Writing Mothers, Writing Daughters: Tracing the Maternal in Stories by American Jewish Women* (Janet Burstein).

- *Becoming a Writer* (Dorothea Brande): The stated goal of the book is to get over yourself and get writing, and she does it with great exercises that are still relevant decades after the book was written.

- Anything written by John Gardner will be both helpful and an inspiration to read: I include here *The Art of Fiction, On Becoming a Novelist, On Writers and Writing, October Light, On Moral Fiction,* and *John Gardner: Literary Outlaw.*

Websites

- Preditors and Editors (anotherealm.com/prededitors): When an agent or publishers sounds a little too good to be true, they probably are. Check them out here.

- Advice for Freelance Writers (writing.org): From a former literary agent and *Playboy* editor, a site with several worthwhile articles for writers.

- Creative Writing Prompts (creativewritingprompts.com): Can't get started? Visit this site for lots of ways to start writing.

- Purdue University's Online Writing Lab (owl.english.purdue.edu): Lots and lots of handouts, a newsletter, and style guides—all at the tip of your fingers.

- One of Us Creative Writing Workshops (oneofus.co.uk): Hints, tips, and advice . . . or try asking a question!

- Creative Writers Podcast (americanwriters.com): If you prefer listening to reading, this site's for you! Take it along in your iPod and keep thinking creatively.

- Writing with Writers (teacher.scholastic.com/writewit/): I *have* to recommend something for getting kids to write, and this site does just that.

- We Feel Fine (wefeelfine.org/): This is an amazing site that explores what's going on in the blogging world right now, through multimedia snippets and captured words. Great place for inspiration.

Blogs

I can't begin to list all the helpful, amusing, enlightening, and fun blogs that are out there concerning writing. It's not accidental: writers are the most prolific bloggers, for obvious reasons. I'm sure that you can locate and read ones that are up your particular literary alley on your own, so I'm confining myself here to listing the ones (that I know of) that may be useful to you in terms of resources:

- The Evil Editor is at evileditor.blogspot.com, and he'll *really* tell you why you're not getting published. Miss Snark and the Evil Editor pull no punches. Not for the faint of heart, but you'll learn a lot.

- DreamTime blogs (dreamtimepublishing.com/blog): As I mentioned in the text, we're all here, so come and chat with us often!

- Beyond the Elements of Style (jeannettecezanne.com): This is my editor Jeannette's blog, filled with seriously good information for writers.

- Ampers & Virgule (ampersandvirgule.blogspot.com): Essays on words and writing. The author does a lot of work with writers wishing to self-publish.

- Writer and editor Susanna J. Sturgis is at susannajsturgis.com/bloggery.php and gives occasional and interesting musings on the writing and editing life.

Index

Absentmindedness, 2–3
Almost Animals (poems), 65–73
Animals, 64–73
Anticipation, 148
Asimov, Isaac, 6, 10, 36

Bailey, Hachaliah, 43
Beatles, 52, 147–148
Behavior, changing of, 104–106
Bell Jar, The, 97
Bertini, Meg, 157
Blink: the Power of Thinking Without Thinking, 110
Blogs, 112, 117, 118–120, 156–157, 166
Book series, 7–8, 151
Books, online, 115
Boyd, Austin, 123–127
Brainstorming, 110–111
Businesses, 110
  Internet, 109–112, 118–119, 133

Byron, George Gordon, Lord Byron, 79

Censorship, of self, 21, 92
Cézanne, Jeannette, 151–154
Chapters, 148
Characters, 11, 30, 33, 48, 63–64, 65, 68, 69, 72–73, 125, 130
Clinton, Bill, 144–145
Collaboration, 44–47, 54–55, 73, 86–93, 150–155
Communication, 82–83, 87, 110–111, 155–156
Confidence, 9, 36, 53
Creativity, 18, 33–34, 45, 98
Critiques and critique groups, 35, 127, 159–160

Da Vinci, Leonardo, 79–80
Diaries, 92–93
Dixon, Franklin W., 6, 8, 10
Drama. *See* Tension and drama.

Dreamtime Publishing, 157
Driving, 1–4, 23–24
Dylan, Bob, 52

Ed Sullivan Show, The (TV
    show), 147
Editors and editorial process,
    111, 113, 126–127, 151–155
Education, elementary, 99,
    100–106
Ed-Vantages (manual), 102–106
Elephants, 42–43
"Elevator pitch," 49
Email, 112
Emotions, 21, 57–58, 77, 81,
    82–83, 111
Experience, 36

Families, 85–93, 102, 103,
    104–106, 130–133, 134–136
Flame Tree, The, 20
Forums, online, 117–118

Generations, 88–90, 131–133,
    144–146
Gladwell, Malcolm, 110
Godin, Seth, 115
Google, 93
Gottlieb, Elaine, 96–98

History, 36
Hobbies, 137

*I Love You Bigger Than an
    Airport*, 86–91
Ideas, 18, 97, 109–110, 118, 122,
    124–125, 137

Images, description of,
    107–108
Individuality, 149, 151,
    155–156
Internet, 109–122
    browsing, 113–115
    links, 113–115, 115–117
    marketing, 118–119
    responsibility for postings,
    111–112, 113, 117–118, 120

Journals, 60, 61

Kennedy, John F., 144–145
Kid's Guide to Relocation, A
    (manual), 134–136
Killing Sea, The, 21

Lewis, Richard, 19–21
Locations. *See* Settings.
Lyrics, 57

Mad Girl's Love Song (poem),
    97
McMurtry, Larry, 137
Memoirs, 36, 139–142
Memory, 108, 142, 143
Mental magnets, 104–105, 148,
    152
Music, 45–46, 51–58
Musicals, 44–47, 55

Note writing, 13–14, 18, 28, 55,
    58–59, 79–80, 108, 110, 130,
    142, 143–144, 146, 148

One Minute Manager, The, 37

Pacing, 38–39
Page, Katherine Hall, 59–61
Perspective, 134–135, 136, 137, 143
Phrasing, 37, 38–39
Plath, Sylvia, 97
Plots, 8, 10–11, 48
Poetry, 12, 37, 125
    Romantic, 31–33, 34, 75–79
Pre-thoughts, 109–111
Pull technology, 120

Quiet House, The (story), 25–27
Quotations. See Sayings.

Reactions, 82–83
Reading, 6–8, 19, 61, 98, 126
    aloud, 38–39
    Internet, 113–115
Relationships, 20, 61, 98, 121–122, 151–155
    parent-children, 85–93, 131–133
Relevance, 67–68
Relocation, 130–136
Roads: Driving America's Great Highways, 137
Rock and roll, 52
RSS feeds, 120

Sayings, 103–104
Schools, 17, 133, 135–136
    extra credit, 16–17
Settings, 12, 29–30, 48
She Walks in Beauty (poem), 78

Signposts. See Sayings.
Simpson, Gail, 102
Solitude, 126, 151, 152–153
Somers, New York, 41, 44, 47
Songs, 12
Songwriting, 45–46, 51–57
Spirituality, 97, 123–124, 126
Stories and storytelling, 24, 28, 29–30, 61, 142–143
Succinctness, 37, 49, 120
Sullivan, Ed, 147–148

Teaching, 41, 43–47, 99–102
Templates, 10–12, 52–53
Tension and drama, 148

Voice, writer's, 152, 155
Wordsworth, William, 76
Writer's block, 30,
Writing, 2–3, 8, 9, 15, 16–17, 19–20, 28, 36, 58, 68, 76, 79–81, 87–88, 92, 97, 120–122, 129–130, 142, 148, 153, 155–156
    exercises and techniques, 10–12, 18, 29–30, 38–39, 48–49, 58–59, 73, 82–83, 93–96, 107–108, 122–123, 137, 147–148
    guides, 160–165
    Internet, 110–122
    interviews about, 19–21, 59–61, 96–98, 123–127
    research for, 93
    resources, 159–166

About the Author

Photo by Regina Madwed, Capitol PhotoInteractive.

Neil Rosen was born in 1947 in Long Beach, New York. He has both a BS and an MS in psychology. He taught elementary school for thirteen years before launching a series of entrepreneurial endeavors. He is currently the founder and CEO of eWay Direct, an e-marketing technology company. Neil is an avid reader, tennis player, bridge player, and—of course!— writer. He enjoys spending time with his three children (Kara, Daniel, and Jenna), his wife Roseann, and his dog Giorgio. He lives and writes in southern Connecticut.

OPEN YOUR HEART

with **Reading**

Mastering Life through
Love of Stories

JEANNETTE CÉZANNE

ONE

Start at the Beginning

Some day you will be old enough
to start reading fairy tales again.

—C. S. LEWIS

The day is dreary and the children are lonely and bored—sent, as were so many young Londoners during World War Two, to live in the country, a supposedly safer environment than the city. Exploring the house, one of them—Lucy—opens a freestanding closet, pushes aside the clothing hanging there, and steps inside, finding herself immediately in a snowy wood. She's stepped through a boundary between worlds, and is now in a kingdom called Narnia.

We could do worse than begin a book about reading with this episode from C. S. Lewis's *The Lion, the Witch, and the Wardrobe.* The reality is that Lucy's experience is perfectly plausible to children who read (or have stories read to them): our earliest experiences of books have us passing over a similar threshold, going through a door that leads to enchantment.

Let's pause for a moment on that threshold and consider what it is that we're doing.

Liminality is a concept popularized by anthropologist Victor Turner, who explored the threshold concept in terms of rituals and rites of passage. The liminal state of being, according to Turner, is ambiguous, open, and uneasy. Beyond it is entry into community, but only through a process that involves danger, change, and—when the individual is considered vis-à-vis the group—exile.

A child following Lucy into the wardrobe is entering the threshold, the twilight zone of liminality. Here he can explore roles and ways of being, safe in the knowledge that he can still turn around and go back out to the bedroom, to the real world. Liminality does not involve commitment: it is a time of uncertainty and growth, of exploration of identity and formation of values.

Liminality is a place where time stands still: when Lucy returns from Narnia, she is teased mercilessly by her brothers and sister, who argue that she has only been gone for a few moments, not for the hours and hours that she experienced beyond the wardrobe. Liminality is dreamtime and has its own rules, its own reality. Dreamtime is every time, and no time, just as it happens in every place and no place.

That dreamtime is no stranger to children. The most magical of stories have a common beginning: "Once upon a time . . ." The Arabic equivalent of this story introduction is even more telling: "It was and was not so . . ."

The other area where liminality is truly part of the literature of childhood is in its clear delineation of boundaries. In many ways, being a child is all about boundaries: creating them, testing them, exploring them, fighting them. Any parent will attest to the need to set clear limits and stick to them, consistently, at whatever the cost: for a child to feel safe, boundaries must remain firm. They must make sense. Venturing into the boundary area is venturing into unknown territory.

And as they test the existence and pliability of boundaries, children also test their meaning. They already know far more about the power of boundaries than we do: what child will dare step on a crack and risk breaking her mother's back?

Many years ago, I worked in the adolescent psychiatric unit of a hospital—a locked unit often used for forensic hospitalizations: the kids there were very sick indeed. One of them, a slight Cambodian girl, was the only member of her family to have survived a mass killing. Her escape from the images of that massacre was sleep—I can still hear her voice, starting around four o'clock in the afternoon: "Go seepy now?"

The corridor was linoleum in a pattern of black and white squares. Maly took an excruciatingly long time to negotiate the squares, stepping carefully in only the white ones . . . but right on the edge, her feet moving with the concentration and grace of a ballet dancer, of a tightrope walker. Some of the unit staff got impatient, exasperated: "Come *on*, Maly!"

I finally thought I understood what she was doing, though. Watching your family hacked to pieces around you is to live in a world dangerously out of control. Even the tight control of the adolescent unit—every minute scheduled and accounted for, checks by staff every five minutes, being unable to do anything independent—wasn't enough for her. As long as she could step carefully enough, she could control that. That one small thing.

She knew a lot about boundaries, did Maly.

Liminality is an important and heady place to visit, but it's not a place to stay—not unless you plan to live on a locked psychiatric unit. We all have to go back through the wardrobe and into the bedroom, face the separation from our parents, face the horror of the war.

And that's what a lot of children's literature explores.

Tell me a story . . .

It's a refrain that's probably as old as the ages. As soon as children learn the magic of stories—their ability to prolong one's awake time, their ability to keep the shadows and the monsters at bay—they also learn the refrain: "Tell me a story."

So much for theory. Pop quiz: what was your favorite childhood book? Bet you named it, quickly and effortlessly, in the same way you could name your favorite stuffed toy.

I remember mine. It was, in retrospect, a fairly horrible book; why my mother thought it would be appropriate is beyond me, and why I read it over and over, obsessively, even though it gave me nightmares—well, that's beyond me, too. But enough about the pathology of my family of origin . . . the name of my book was *The Tall Book of Make-Believe,* and not only did it have scary stories in it, it had even scarier pictures, including one of a tree with eyes and a predatory expression and another of a child being flattened to drag under a door.

Like it or not, that was "my" first book of any significance. (Oddly enough, it has since then become a collector's item, for reasons that elude me. I no longer had my old copy, but Paul very sweetly searched for it and secured a copy for me—for money that would have absolutely amazed my mother.)

I was determined that my stepchildren would have a better first-book experience than I'd had, and, as luck would have it, I was working as a community relations manager for a bookstore (trying to get a sense of what people read, as a matter of fact) when Paul and I first met.

Of course, I knew nothing about children. My first attempt to engage them in reading went a few steps down my mother's path—I'd fallen in love with Graeme Base's pop-up version of Lewis Carroll's *Jabberwocky,* and proposed making a gift of it. Paul took one look at the pictures, with their swirling colors and sharp teeth and scaled creatures and gently nixed the idea.

Back to the drawing-board.

I'd by then volunteered to do a reading time that we offered in the children's section of the bookshop, and found that my favorite books were ones I could read dramatically—unsure of myself around children, I needed all the help I could get. These books allowed me to get past my child-phobia and really relax into a role.

And that was how I met the Wapiti-Hoo.

It was Wapiti-Hoo, for I saw him
Riding a moonbeam ray
Out towards the mists and shadows
That hovered about the bay
Out towards the playful ripples
Out o'er the waters blue
And the hills that rise in the misty light
Sent back his name as he took his flight:
Wapiti, Wapiti-Hoo!

It was Wapiti-Hoo, for he called me
While I was watching a star
Called while the star was telling me
A message it brought from afar
Out beyond old Orion
Where the skies are forever new
And the words that came when I heard
   his call
Echoed afar through the starlit hall,
Wapiti, Wapiti-Hoo!

It was Wapiti-Hoo, for I know him
He comes to play with me here
Comes in the evening moonlight
When no one else is near,
Skips and leaps in the shadows,
Bathes in the sparkling dew
And he loves me most when I love him best
And says "Good-night" when I go to rest
Wapiti, Wapiti-Hoo!
(Night-Night.)